Le Corbusier

on camera

Le Corbusier on camera

The unknown films of Ernest Weissmann

Veronique Boone

with a foreword by Tim Benton

Birkhäuser
Basel

THIS PUBLICATION WAS MADE POSSIBLE BY THE KIND SUPPORT OF

Faculté d'Architecture La Cambre Horta
Université de Lille
Fondation Le Corbusier
Delen Private Bank

PROJECT MANAGEMENT
Henriette Mueller-Stahl, Berlin

LAYOUT, COVER DESIGN, TYPESETTING AND LITHOGRAPHY
Gunther Fobe, Gent

COPY EDITING
Ian McDonald, Solva

PRODUCTION
Anja Haering, Berlin

PAPER
Munken Lynx, 150 g/m^2

PRINTING
DZA Druckerei zu Altenburg GmbH

COVER ILLUSTRATIONS

Library of Congress Control Number: 2023943813

Bibliographic information published by the German National Library
The German National Library lists this publication in the Deutsche Nationalbibliografie; detailed bibliographic data are available on the Internet at http://dnb.dnb.de.

ISBN 978-3-0356-2728-2

Hardcover ISBN 978-3-0356-2729-9
Special edition ISBN 978-3-0356-2730-5
e-ISBN (PDF) 978-3-0356-2787-9

Im Westfeld 8
4055 Basel
Switzerland
Part of Walter de Gruyter GmbH, Berlin/Boston

9 8 7 6 5 4 3 2 1

www.birkhauser.com

Table of contents

Foreword

by Tim Benton

Le Corbusier and Pierre Jeanneret had worked with various draughtsmen in the 1920s – and notably with Pierre Emery, who worked intensively on the Quartier Moderne Frugès at Pessac – but it was the competition for the Palace of the League of Nations, in the winter of 1926–1927, that brought about the first large-scale introduction of international architects to the rue de Sèvres. From then on, the atelier was always full of young men and women who were drawn to the flame of Le Corbusier's reputation. Many of them – such as Albert Frey, Josep Lluís Sert, Kunio Maekawa, Junzo Sakakura, Alfred Roth, and Charlotte Perriand – went on to establish themselves as leading modern architects around the world.

There is a log book of the presentation drawings made by these assistants dating from 4 April 1925. The first eleven pages are missing. From 7 February 1929 (page 26 verso of the "black book"), a column is labelled "dessinateur!" (draughtsman!) – and the first name we find is that of Ernest Weissmann.

Life in the rue de Sèvres was not always easy. We know from the witness of Alfred Roth, for example, how difficult was his position as site architect in Stuttgart during the construction of the two houses at the Weissenhof Siedlung in 1927.[1] Roth also recounts how, after the competition drawings for the League of Nations project had finally been sent off, Le Corbusier hired a coach and took them all for a trip to Chartres. At the end of the dinner, he made a rousing speech about how architecture was carried by the enthusiasm of the young, before admitting that he was not proposing to pay them. Eventually he relented and offered some of them, at least, the price of a ticket home.

Although Le Corbusier and Pierre Jeanneret helped form a certain way of thinking among their young collaborators, the influences ran both ways. It is noticeable, for example, that the use of axonometric projections became more frequent after 1927. To give just one example, Norman Rice, trained in the Beaux-Arts system with Paul Cret in Philadelphia, drew axonometric projections for the de Beistegui apartment.[2] It is also true that some of the assistants were able to carry out projects that had eluded the master. For example, the Casa Bloc in Barcelona (1932–1936) was the first recognizable execution of Le Corbusier's Ville Radieuse scheme. Josep Lluís Sert, who worked at the rue de Sèvres on and off from 1927 to 1929, was the link. Another example is the block of flats High Point One at Highgate, London (1933–1935) by the Russian architect Berthold Lubetkin, who worked briefly with Le Corbusier. Le Corbusier inaugurated the building and wrote an article celebrating it as a breakthrough in 1936.[3] At the *Exposition Internationale des Arts et Techniques dans la Vie Moderne* in Paris in 1937, two of Le Corbusier's former assistants built important pavilions (Sakakura for Japan and Sert for the Spanish Republic). Although the design of the Yugoslav Pavilion was won in competition by Joseph Seissel, Weissmann played a part in its construction.

1. Hélène Cauquil and Marc Bedarida, "Le Corbusier. L'Atelier 35 rue de Sèvres", *Bulletin d'Informations Architecturales de l'IFA*, Summer 1987. See also A. Roth, *Amusante Erlebnisse eines Architekten* (Zurich: gta/Ammann) 1988, 18.

2. E.g. FLC 17436 (LC 2245, 14/11/1929), FLC 17439 (LC 2248, 30/11/1929), and FLC 17440 (LC 2273, 8/1/1930).

3. Le Corbusier, "The vertical garden city by Le Corbusier [pseud]", *Architectural Review*, 79, 1936, 9-10.

Introduction

***Passages de vie* at 35, rue de Sèvres**
The unknown amateur films of Ernest Weissmann.
A backdrop to architectural history

by Veronique Boone

Architect and development planner Ernest Weissmann.
An international civil servant

by Tamara Bjažić Klarin

Passages de vie at 35, rue de Sèvres
The unknown amateur films of Ernest Weissmann. A backdrop to architectural history

by Veronique Boone

Ernest Weissmann with his camera at the building site of the Villa Savoye, May 1929

In 1929, soon after arriving at the Atelier Le Corbusier and Pierre Jeanneret at 35, rue de Sèvres, the Croatian architect Ernest Weissmann – a "charming boy", as Le Corbusier describes him to his mother – acquires the new amateur 9.5 mm film camera made by Pathé. The Atelier is a very vibrant place at this time, and its reputation is growing as it obtains for the first time large-scale projects, a process which is reflected in the influx of foreign collaborators. The enthusiasm and the feeling of the exceptional experience at 35, rue de Sèvres prompts Weissmann to capture these moments on film, offering what are today unknown stories behind the canonical architecture history of modernism.

In the introduction of the second volume of the *Œuvre complète*, Le Corbusier wrote about the turn of the decade 1929–1930 that "this year meant to me, to a certain extent, the end of a long period of research for us. 1930 inaugurated a new stage of preoccupations: the great works, the great events of architecture and town planning, the prodigious era of the equipment of a new machine-based civilisation".[1] Most of the Parisian villas were built, such as the Villa La Roche-Jeanneret, the Villa Planeix, the Villa Cook, and the Villa Stein-de Monzie. The two pavilions of the Villa Church were completed, and the ongoing project for the Villa Savoye had become a reality. The Cité Frugès, an experimental settlement of 50 workers' houses in Pessac near Bordeaux, was achieved in 1927 and, after first-year problems with the utility services, finally occupied. The competition for the Palace of the League of Nations in Geneva, and the debacle created by the opaque decision to disqualify Le Corbusier and Pierre Jeanneret, occupied the Atelier between 1926 and 1928. It put Le Corbusier definitively on the international map as one of the most prominent architectural figures and led, in June 1928, to the foundation of the CIAM, the Congrès Internationaux d'Architecture Moderne (International Congress of Modern Architecture) in La Sarraz to plead the cause of the new architecture, with Le Corbusier as one of the initiators. The architecture projects Le Corbusier and Pierre Jeanneret obtained shifted in scale. The studies for the Maison Clarté in Geneva for the contractor Edmond Wanner were ongoing, as were, since 1928, the studies for the Centrosoyus project in Moscow, prompting several visits by Le Corbusier to the Russian capital. The commission for the Cité de Refuge of the Salvation Army was signed in 1929 after the Atelier had already carried out the construction of its Palais du Peuple in 1926 and the reconversion project for the Asile Flottant, completed in 1929; the project for the Pavillon Suisse student housing at the Cité Universitaire in Paris was assigned to the architects in 1930. Le Corbusier

1. Boesiger, Willy and Oscar Stonorov, eds. *Le Corbusier et Pierre Jeanneret. Œuvre complète 1929-1934*. (Zurich: Girsberger, 1935), 11.

Perspective of the Centrosoyus project for Moscow, 1929

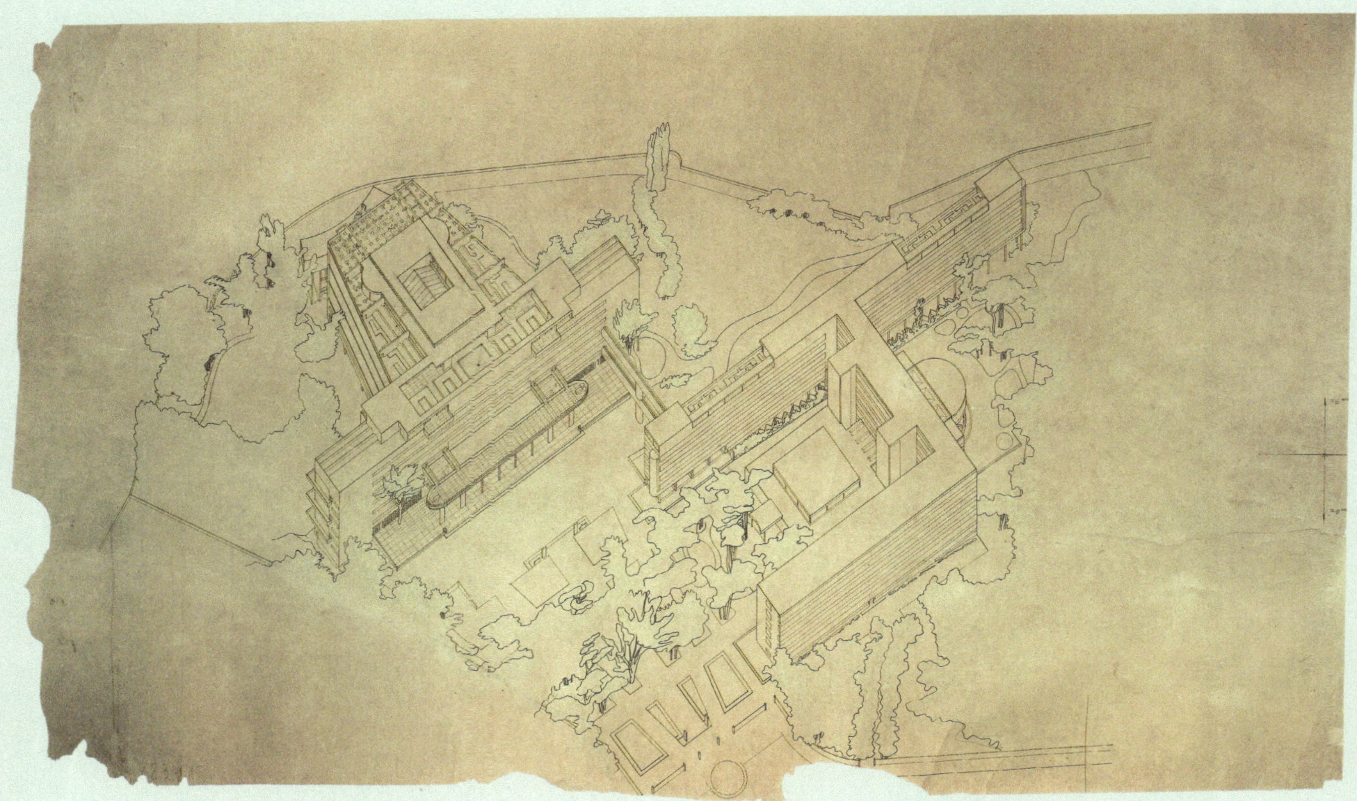

Axonometric drawing of the project for the Palace of the League of Nations competition in Geneva, 1927

continued his reflections on the modern city after having presented his Plan for a City of 3 Million Inhabitants at the Salon d'Automne in 1922 and his Plan Voisin for Paris in the L'Esprit Nouveau Pavilion at the International Exhibition of Modern Decorative and Industrial Arts in 1925. Further research would culminate a few years later in works and proposals for urban-planning projects – for example, that of the Rive Gauche in Antwerp in 1933. The growing celebrity status of Le Corbusier was reflected in invitations to international conferences, and assisted by his numerous writings. In the autumn of 1929, he travelled for two months to South America for ten lectures on architecture and urbanism, which he published the following year in *Précisions*.[2] Finally, in September 1929, Le Corbusier also completed the manuscript of what was to become the first volume of a series of eight of the *Œuvre complète*.

Le Corbusier and Pierre Jeanneret could benefit from the enthusiasm of young architects from all over the world who wanted to join one of the most avant-garde architecture offices of that time. When Weissmann arrived at the Atelier Le Corbusier and Pierre Jeanneret, it was experiencing its first expansion. Amongst the collaborators at that moment, with many names that became well known afterwards, there was Charlotte Perriand for the furniture and interior design since 1927; Alfred Roth, who arrived the same year from Switzerland until summer 1928; and Kunio Maekawa from Japan, who arrived in 1928. The American Norman Rice, the Swiss Albert Frey, and the Spanish Josep Lluís Sert all arrived with Ernest Weissmann around mid-1928. The Russian Nikolai Kolli arrived in 1929, spending his time between Paris and Moscow. During his internship in the Atelier, Weissmann worked on several of those large-scale projects: the second project for the Palace of the League of Nations in Geneva, the execution plans of the Cité de Refuge in Paris, and the execution plans and details of the Centrosoyus project in Moscow.[3] He also was in charge of the classification of the photographic collection and the processing of requests for photographs from the Atelier. The collaborators shared an enthusiasm for the exceptional working environment, visits to emblematic building sites, and events in the city. Some photographic memories of evenings at the Atelier testify to the coherence and enthusiasm that bound the collaborators together. Lifelong friendships were created during this period between collaborators who would later go on to have important and international careers, but they also kept in contact with their masters on numerous occasions.

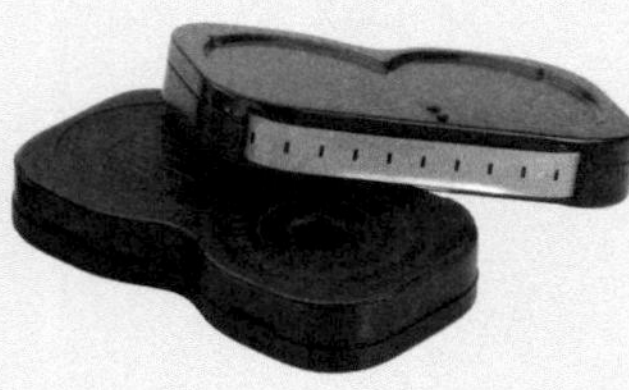

Motocaméra Pathé-Lux model of 1928, with its spring motor and double cassette, as used by Weissmann

Aware of the exceptionality of the experience at the Atelier, Weissmann would use his newly acquired 9.5 Pathé Baby Motocaméra to capture the experiences and events he was witnessing with his colleagues and friends. This motorized camera model was launched at the end of 1928, five years after the first introduction of a manual amateur camera by Charles Pathé in spring 1923. The compact film camera is described in its manual as "elegant, precise and robust". Measuring 12 by 12 cm with a thickness of only 6 cm, the camera fits easily in one hand – offering handheld filming. The new model Weissmann bought was equipped with a spring motor, offering more flexible handling freedom, and was a big step forward from the first model, where the film had to be rotated manually. The introduction of this first compact amateur film camera in 1923 came barely six months after the

2. Le Corbusier, *Précisions sur un état présent de l'architecture et de l'urbanisme* (Paris: Les Éditions G. Crès & Cie, 1930).

3. Le Corbusier, Certificat, 5 November 1930, FLC, R3-7-486.

Publicity in the magazine *La Photo pour tous* (March 1929) on the use of the Pathé Motocaméra for leisure and journeys

launch of the 9.5 mm inflammable silver film "Baby Pathé" for Christmas 1922, with a manually operated projector and a catalogue of titles from the Pathé Film Library including short cuts of major films distributed in cinemas, documentaries and animations as well as newsreels filmed by the Pathé Gazette, to be projected at home – so creating the first home cinema.[4] The new film format of 9.5 mm was from the beginning imagined as an affordable format, as was the amateur camera. As one 35 mm film can hold three 9.5 mm films, the calculation of the economic gain is rapidly done. The perforations of the 9.5 mm films are positioned in the centre of the film, in between the individual images, so that the image could use the whole width of the film and benefit from the highest possible quality. For the two existing formats of the time, 16 mm and 35 mm, the perforations are typically situated at the edges of the film, limiting the size of the sensitive image. The 9.5 mm format could thus offer quality almost equal to the 16 mm at a significantly lower price. Projecting and filming were done at 16 frames per second – which is much lower than the actual 24 images per second. As a film reel measured about 9 metres, this resulted in a total projection time of about 1 minute 15 seconds. To compensate for the problem of the short duration, the projector could be stopped during intertitles or a fixed shot to increase the total duration of projecting. The camera had an easy-loading system for the double cassette wherein the same film reel, with its short length of 9 metres, was held. The mechanics also allowed filming

4. Anne Gourdet-Mares, "La caméra Pathé-Baby: Le cinéma amateur à l'âge de l'expérimentation", in *L'amateur de cinéma: Un autre paradigme: Histoire, esthétique, marges et institutions*, ed. Valérie Vignaux and Benoît Turquety, Histoire Culturelle (Paris: Afrhc, 2017), 74–93.

at an increased or decreased speed to manipulate a better light exposure for the film. The camera was equipped with a 20 mm 3.5 lens. This being the first handheld amateur camera, its instruction manual leads the user through the apprehension of filming with simple tricks, such as fixed framing for a moving subject, the drawing with chalk of the film frame on the floor, required distances, how to move the camera, necessary speed, etc. A whole new world was opening up for the amateur filmmaker, and he or she needed to be instructed. The distinction between professional and amateur is clearly made by always showing the Pathé Baby camera with a woman. The assumption was: if a woman can operate it, anyone can! Hence, Pathé offered a complete film experience: camera, film and projection apparatus, accompanied by the Pathé Film Library catalogue. The simple handling of the projector and camera; the affordable cost of camera, film, and projector; and the good quality of film contributed to their rapid success. Distributed throughout Europe, including Britain, the 9.5 mm format was produced until the mid-1960s, when it was finally pushed out of the market by the 16 mm and 8 mm formats.

Weissmann filmed more than one hour of footage between 1929 and the mid-1930s. This means that, on average, he bought a film cartridge almost every month. The first filmed sequences taken by Weissmann that have been conserved and identified were taken around May 1929. The last images in Paris were taken a year later, in late spring. In this period of just over a year, Weissmann filmed more than 20 minutes of events at the Atelier, with Le Corbusier and Pierre Jeanneret and with his close colleagues, and covered the whole construction of the Villa Savoye. Weissmann's film footage offers an original document on the working environment of the Atelier and its mode of organization. Weissmann witnesses, together with Pierre Jeanneret, Le Corbusier's first trip by plane; he visits the Villa Stein-de Monzie with his friends; films a working meeting between Le Corbusier and Pierre Jeanneret; participates in the creation of the Mundaneum diorama; accompanies art critic and friend Sigfried Giedion on his visits to Paris and the construction sites of the Villa Savoye and the Asile Flottant barge of the Salvation Army; visits the Salon de l'Automobile; and is present at the fourth CIAM congress in Athens in 1933. These are sequences taken on the spot, in contrast to the well-known professional photographs that were taken of the projects of Le Corbusier and Pierre Jeanneret. Through his camera, Weissmann achieves an intimate and informal view of Le Corbusier and Pierre Jeanneret in their work and activities, and reveals the convivial relationships with the other collaborators. The desire to capture these unique occasions shows how Weissmann experienced the time at the Atelier as a decisive moment in his life.

Poster on the easy use – by a woman – of the Motocaméra Pathé-Lux, 1928

After leaving the Atelier in October 1930, Weissmann continued to use his camera during the 1930s to film models and projects of his own professional career, such as the competition model for the Foundation Block at Zagreb that he designed in 1929 with Norman Rice and Kunio Maekawa with close references to the Centrosoyus building, capturing the burning of the model after losing the competition; the Sokol sports centre in Pisarovina, which was completed in 1931; or the disassembled model of the 1931–1932 project for the Press Centre with National Theatre hall in Belgrade. Apart from capturing the events of his professional life, Weissmann abundantly filmed his leisure activities – skiing, mountain climbing, swimming, motorbike competitions, soccer games, visits to car exhibitions, etc. – which he did in the company of his masters; his close colleagues; friends and family; and his future wife, Ingeborg. Most of these films remain unexplored. Weissmann continued to film his professional activities after settling in New York in 1939 – for example, the construction of Richard Buckminster Fuller's Dymaxion House at the Museum of Modern Art (MoMA), in which he participated. The films of his first years in New York were marked by a professionalization: he changed his film format to a 16 mm camera "Bell & Howell Filmo 70D" and used colour film most of the time. This parallels his activities as a professional photographer for a photographic agency in New York during 1940–1942. His numerous photographs and the catalogues of his images show a person of many qualities, little known until today. On one single occasion, at the *Image of Freedom* exhibition held at the MoMA in New York during winter 1941–1942, the portrait photograph of a worker at the market that he submitted was awarded. Taken on the spot, the photograph is representative of the amateur viewpoint that was already apparent in his films.

Weissmann kept his 9.5 mm amateur films as raw material; no cutting has been done or montage or intertitles added – even if Pathé provided all apparatuses to do so and despite, for example, the repetitive filming of the Villa Savoye. The sequences seen today are as they were filmed: sometimes blurred or jerky, with long or very short sequences. Several sequences show Weissmann himself – proof that he also lent the camera to his colleagues. Some films have different shades of yellow, graininess, or flow stains – indications that Weissmann developed his films himself, or at least did so for some reels. The sequences show a gradual mastering of the use of the camera. The reels include elegant framing, fine compositions, and remarkable scenes. Weissmann's primary aims in using the camera were to record, to manipulate a new technology, and to experiment with its possibilities – in short, to act as a home-movie filmmaker.[5] The filmed sequences reveal much about the way Weissmann looked through the film camera. His constant concern about

Opposite page: Unrolled part of a film reel of Weissmann's, which probably depicts his wife, Ingeborg

5. Roger Odin, "La question de l'amateur dans trois espaces de réalisation et de diffusion", *Communications* 68, Le cinéma en amateur, 1999, 47–89.

Ascent shot of the ramp at the Villa Savoye by Pierre Chenal, from *Architecture d'aujourd'hui*, 1931

framing confirms his interest and experience in photography. The film footage can be seen merely as moving photographs rather than film. By filming, Weissmann does not act, nor he is considering himself, as a filmmaker but rather as a photographer capturing moments he would otherwise maybe take in photographs. He is not looking for a narrative but for the uniqueness of the events. Just as László Moholy-Nagy referred to some shots of his 1933 film *Architect's Diary* on the CIAM event that year as "family shots", the filmed events of Weissmann refer to the intimate circle of friendship, as the professional and the amicable were heavily intertwined. But instead of creating a photographic album, in which the pictures can be seen in chronological order of the events, this footage is a loose collections of film reels with, at best, the event or a date written on the box. The chronological order of events in the life of a young architect do not have any importance, but the events in themselves that have been filmed are at the centre of attention. The often careful framing of the sequences and their subject, as well as the duality with the playfulness of the new "toy", are the main reasons to reproduce here the filmed material as photographs.

Among Weissmann's experimentations with the camera, a visit to the Villa Stein-de Monzie with his close colleagues is appealing for the comprehension of a cinematic view versus an architectural view. Weissmann films, with camera in hand, the ascent of the spiral staircase of the Villa Stein-de Monzie. He films from the point of view of an architect as he climbs the stairs: on a walk. The result is a very hectic, blurred image that constantly rotates during the ascent. It is a literal realization of the architectural walk, which demonstrates that cinema needs another way of representation to visualize the idea of the *promenade architecturale*. By identifying the camera's eye with the human eye, the captured image becomes

Film still from a sequence on the *Graf Zeppelin*, filmed by Le Corbusier when he travelled to Rio de Janeiro from Frankfurt am Main, July 1936

very restricted: moving, blurred, and dark as a result of the limitations of the film, the sensitivity to light, and the framing. This sequence reflects an ignorance of the cinematic codes and techniques of presenting movement through architecture in film, which is to externalize the camera from the filmed movement – as seen, for example, with the visits to the villas in Pierre Chenal's *Architecture d'aujourd'hui* of 1931. Chenal also films the staircase of the Villa Stein-de Monzie but the movement is captured by a person on the stairs, with a fixed camera.

In addition to the reels filmed by Weissmann, some contain documentary films from the Pathé Film Library, such as *Bridges and viaducts*, *Transformers*, *The Acropolis*, *New York* and *Port of Dunkirk: the tooling*. The presence of these films shows that Weissmann also made use of the Pathé film catalogue, with its selection of technical documentaries, and that film viewing was certainly more common in Le Corbusier's entourage than one would think – even if the archives lack evidence of the acquisition of a projector. Indeed, in Le Corbusier's collection of 16 mm films shot between 1936 and 1938 by himself, there is also a small slapstick film. Although the Weissmann archives held a cheap Ciné-Gel 9.5 mm projector of the 1940s, no projector of the 1920s has been found. But it seems more than likely that Weissmann also owned a "Baby Pathé" projector, as he otherwise could not view the films in his possession provided from the Pathé catalogue.

This taste for film in the early decades of the medium's existence is not confined to Weissmann. Internationally, avant-garde architects embraced film and cinema as a new modern art and technique, discussed in their magazines – for example, by Le Corbusier and Amédée Ozenfant in *L'Esprit nouveau*, but also by others in *MA*, *Blaue Reiter*, *Merz*, and *7 Arts*. The admiration for this new technique was not limited to theoretical discussions; the portable camera formats that came

VARIÉTÉS

TŒPFFER

PRÉCURSEUR DU CINÉMA

PAR

DE FAYET

Extrait de l'Histoire du Dr Festus.

TŒPFFER PRÉCURSEUR DU CINÉMA 1337

SI LE MOT AVAIT EXISTÉ, TŒPFFER, EN 1830, *EUT ÉCRIT EN SOUS-TITRE A SES ALBUMS* : « HISTOIRE DE M. CRÉPIN », *AVENTURES CINÉMATOGRAPHIQUES*, « HISTOIRE DE M. PENSIL », *COMÉDIE CINÉMATOGRAPHIQUE* », etc., etc.

Le cinéma est un outil merveilleux qui est fait pour nous procurer tous les enchantements. Les éléments lui appartiennent, l'eau, la terre, l'espace. Point de limites à ses prétentions : l'agencement du *studio* permet toutes les fabrications. Les lois de la pesanteur ne le gênent pas, ni celles du temps. Avec le « ralenti », des sensations physiques, profondément troublantes, nous arrachent de notre univers. La distance n'existe plus. Le ciné résout le possible et l'impossible.

Si le public savait comment on fabrique un film, du coup ses exigences se manifesteraient. Le public qui sait comment on fait la bonne cuisine, prétend avoir du plaisir à table ; il prétendrait s'amuser mieux au ciné qu'au théâtre Cluny.

L'homme a toujours aimé le merveilleux ; les poètes le lui ont décrit. Mais aujourd'hui, le ciné peut du *merveilleux plausible*, alerte, comme la plus folle rêverie ; il donne la possibilité d'y croire ; il vous arrache à la réalité.

Le ciné peut être Gargantua comme il peut être Ali Baba. Mais il peut bien davantage. Après avoir employé les hommes, les paysages, l'air, la mer, il peut, par le dessin animé, montrer les genèses les plus inattendues ; il peut, par des constructions géométriques successives, régler des virtualités impressionnantes, jusqu'ici inconcevables.

La poésie n'est pas dans les mots aux significations perturbées dans lesquels se débattent aujourd'hui les poètes. La poésie est dans le rapport des faits.

Le cinéma nous ennuie à mourir avec ses reconstitutions littéraires, ses épisodes, ses histoires d'amour et d'argent. Charlot qui a triomphé partout le prouve bien. Le ciné ne doit pas se livrer à des reconstitutions réalistes ; Zola était suffisant en imprimé. Il nous torture sur le film.

***

Rodolphe Tœpffer, maitre de pension à Genève, au début du siècle passé, a dessiné l'histoire de plusieurs héros, Crépin, Vieux-Bois, Festus, Pensil.

La manière dont il a agencé son dessin et les légendes constitue un véritable film. Les vignettes se succèdent comme les feuillets des petits cinés en carnet qu'on effeuillait il y a vingt ans. Mais son invention cinégraphique véritable, c'est sa conception de l'intrigue. Il joue avec des hommes et des femmes, des animaux, avec des sentiments stéréotypés et il s'emporte en des fantaisies folles, passant au delà des réalités possibles et créant un monde plausible dont il a désarticulé les fatales règles. Ses personnages n'ont plus faim, ne sont plus sujets aux petites réglementations quotidiennes, vivent dans l'air, dans l'eau, ne meurent jamais à la suite d'événements fabuleux, mais meurent plus tard quand tout est fini, comme tout le monde, dans leur lit ; leur intelligence n'est plus occupée de multiples pensées simultanées, mais galvanisée sur un seul point : l'intrigue en cours. Ce sont des hommes, c'est nous-mêmes en effigies décisives. Si Rabelais avait l'esprit énorme, Tœpffer l'eut aigu.

Quand je suis au cinéma où je me désespère, je songe à Tœpffer. Son dessin, du reste, était exquis, exceptionnel. Il faisait cela pour amuser ses élèves et ne songeait pas qu'il était un grand artiste. Gœthe, en voyage, de passage à Genève, vit Tœpffer et ses dessins et il exigea de lui qu'il les publiât.

De Fayet.

The first article that Le Corbusier and Amédée Ozenfant published in *L'Esprit nouveau*, November 1921, on their thoughts on cinema; although written by Ozenfant, Toepffer was a reference shared by both

onto the market led practitioners to try it out. The first professional, portable 35 mm camera, a Zeiss Kinamo, was to have a profound effect on film practices – leading to a less static use of the filmed view and more fragmented editing due to the constraints of the short reels of this portable equipment. Sergei Eisenstein, László Moholy-Nagy and Joris Ivens are just a few examples of filmmakers who put the new possibilities offered by this camera to work. The amateur cameras followed this evolution by aiming to bring the practice of filmmaking within the reach of everyone. Marcel Lods, Léon Stynen, Jaap Bakema, Carl Hubacher, Rudolf Steiger, and Le Corbusier all applied themselves to the new technique during the 1930s – but so did personalities such as Hélène de Mandrot, who hosted the first International Congress of Modern Architecture (CIAM) at her home in La Sarraz in 1928 and the following year, in 1929, the first International Congress of Independent Filmmakers (CICI), with the same type of 9.5 mm camera that Weissmann used shortly afterwards. If, in the mid-1930s, the use of a semi-amateur camera seems to have been taken for granted in the avant-garde community of architects, Weissmann seems to have been ahead of his colleagues. It is likely that Le Corbusier became interested in film through Ernest Weissmann's use of the 9.5 mm camera, but it would take until 1936 before Le Corbusier experienced it himself.[6]

6. Tim Benton, *LC Foto: Le Corbusier: Secret Photographer* (Zurich: Lars Müller, 2013).

The surviving films are conserved today at the Fondation Le Corbusier in Paris and at the Ubu Gallery in New York. An undated montage of the various films on Weissmann's period at the Atelier on four large Pathex reels, each 18 cm in diameter, has removed the original metal cartridges as well as any indication of Weissmann's hand, and has eradicated original sources on the film's production. The recent frame-by-frame digitalization of the 9.5 mm films from the period at the Atelier Le Corbusier and Pierre Jeanneret reveals all the richness and beauty of both the documentary and the framing aspects. The sequences filmed indoors – for example, at the Atelier – or during the painting weekend for the Mundaneum diorama, are often underexposed, explained by their long hidden life without being viewed. It is only today that with the merits of the digitalization, offering the possibility to adjust the images, all the details of these captured events can be fully enjoyed. The raw material of the digitalized films had to be timed and cut, dated, located, and the filmed subjects recognized and identified. Evident and less-evident elements present in the images gave clues concerning dates and places: tree foliage; dress code; the constructions, buildings, and streets filmed; the people present in the film; the nature of the events; indications of publicity; etc. The images were cross-referenced with other archival sources, especially from the archives of Ernest Weissmann and the Le Corbusier archives, such as family correspondence, diaries and notebooks, progress reports on the constructions, dated plans, etc. – but also other archives such as the Norman Rice Collection, the Josep Lluís Sert archive, the Paul Otlet archive, and the Sigfried Giedion archive, as well as scanning the popular press of the time. The cross-referencing of these sources made it possible to date most of the professional visits and events Weissmann captured during his stay in the Paris Atelier. The leisure activities such as the bathing or skiing, which took on a more generic character, were impossible to clearly identify and date. Some sources, such as Le Corbusier's correspondence with his mother and wife, or with Paul Otlet, are revealing not only in terms of dating the filmed scenes but, above all, in terms of obtaining additional information about the events and better defining their temporal framework. For example, Le Corbusier tells his mother and Paul Otlet about the creation of the Mundaneum diorama during a hot weekend, and he also describes to his mother and wife his nausea during the flight to Cologne – elements that make it possible to date these events and to know their personal impact for Le Corbusier.

Few personal elements have been preserved in the archives of Ernest Weissmann, but the care he took in carrying his films with him through the different periods he moved from Zagreb to Paris, London, and New York prove the importance for Weissmann of this visual archive. Through the time that Weissmann took to film certain events, we can see the importance that these events had for him. While the writings of Weissmann are not witness to how he lived in this period, his films are the record of this exceptional experience that would influence his later career.

One of the small iron boxes for the film reels used by Weissmann, which he kept carefully his whole life

Architect and development planner Ernest Weissmann. An international civil servant

by Tamara Bjažić Klarin

Ernest Weissmann was an architect, development planner, and public servant deeply committed to making the world a better place for the oppressed. For this reason, Weissmann redefined the span of professional engagements of architects and urban planners. Faced with social problems, housing shortages, and town crises, he envisioned architecture and planning as complex social activities that were based on scientific engineering, consideration for the broader social and economic context, and the level of technological advancement in society. Architects, he believed, should work in accordance with the demands of rationalization, standardization, and prefabrication. Similarly, urban planning must ensure sustainable development by achieving balance between the city and its surroundings, and by considering existing and potential living conditions. Those beliefs, formed at the very beginning of his career, were the basis of his continually expanding field of work – from a building, the city, and its region to state-wide and continental regional planning in Asia, Latin America, and Africa. The peak of Weissmann's career was the Habitat Charter, a set of guidelines for solving the global housing crisis and uncontrolled urbanization through joint national economic and social-housing planning and a more equitable distribution of the benefits of development. The set of skills that allowed him to easily adjust the scope and scale of his professional endeavours – from a freelance architect in Zagreb to a manager of the United Nations' (UN's) Department of Housing, Building and Planning – were honed over the years through self-education and by working with prominent figures such as Le Corbusier and in international organizations such as the CIAM and the UN. Whether by chance or on purpose, Weissmann always seemed to be in the right place at the right time.

Model of the Foundation Hospital Pavilion for Tuberculosis, part of the Foundation and Clinical Hospital in Zagreb international competition, 1930–31

Competition design by Ernest Weissmann, Kunio Maekawa, and Norman Rice of the Foundation Block in Zagreb, 1929: the project was influenced by the Centrosoyus and Salvation Army Cité de Refuge projects, on which the collaborators worked at 35, rue de Sèvres.

Meeting Le Corbusier and *Neues Bauen* architects

Weissmann graduated in architecture from the Technical Faculty in Zagreb in 1926. His thesis project was "a house for workers' welfare", designed in the style of modernized neoclassicism typical of Zagreb's School of Architecture. Thanks to fellow Croatian architect Zlatko Neumann, an assistant of Adolf Loos in Vienna and Paris, Weissmann moved in 1927 to Paris to pursue professional training in the architecture studios of Adolf Loos, and Le Corbusier and Pierre Jeanneret until 1930. In the Atelier Le Corbusier and Pierre Jeanneret, he joined a creative international environment: a group of young architects from Europe, America, and Asia eager to learn about new architecture – Albert Frey, Charlotte Perriand, Norman Rice, Kunio Maekawa, and Josep Lluís Sert. They acquired valuable knowledge on flexible and economic ways of designing and building with skeletal construction and non-load-bearing walls that enabled the free disposition of spaces. Weissmann learned new "tools" by working on Le Corbusier's and Pierre Jeanneret's major projects in the 1920s – the Villa Savoye in Poissy, the Cité de Refuge in Paris, and the Centrosoyus in Moscow. His personal mission was to introduce the new architecture to Yugoslavia, on which he worked systematically by participating in architectural competitions from 1928 onwards. With that goal in mind, he returned to Zagreb in 1930, where he became one of the best-known architects of his generation due to the awards he received in international competitions for the Jewish Hospital and the Foundation and Clinical Hospital – both in Zagreb.

The focus of Weissmann's work from 1928 to 1930 was a new type of prefabricated hospital building with skeletal construction developed through several projects – the Sanatorium for the Tuberculosis of Bones and Joints in Kraljevica and competition designs for Zagreb hospitals. Weissmann's design concept of the time was influenced by the European leftist architects gathered at the Bauhaus school of design in Dessau, and in Frankfurt am Main. They argued for the typified and prefabricated social housing to which Weissmann was introduced during the second CIAM congress in Frankfurt in 1929 on the "Minimum Dwelling". Weissmann felt close to the leftists' programme formulated in CIAM's Declaration from its foundation in La Sarraz the year before. According to this programme, the architect was an engineer: a socially responsible and engaged individual whose task was to use architecture as a tool of social change. The task of architecture was to solve social problems by using modern technologies in the construction of mass housing and public facilities. For Weissmann – who used photography and film, drove cars and motorcycles – the new technology was the reality. He presented the programme of *new architecture* in Yugoslavia on two occasions – in the publication on the Sanatorium for the Tuberculosis of Bones and Joints in 1930, and by publishing the translation of CIAM's Declaration in the book *The Problems of Contemporary Architecture* in 1932.[1] This book was a joint effort of the new generation of Zagreb- and Belgrade-based architects. With this move, Weissmann enlisted them among supporters of the Congress.

Film still with two collaborators of Ernest Weissmann holding the model of the Belgrade Press Centre with the National Theatre Hall, 1931; the structure of the Hall is reminiscent of that of the Centrosoyus project.

1. Stjepan Planić, *Problemi savremene arhitekture* (Zagreb: Jugoslovenska štampa, 1932).

The new CIAM's leftist architects and regional planning

From 1932, CIAM had a crucial role in Weissmann's international activities. He founded the Zagreb Work Group, a socially engaged architectural group, and the Yugoslav national group within CIAM. For the fourth CIAM Congress, on the "Functional City" in 1933, the group created analytical maps of the residential, occupational, and transportation infrastructure of Zagreb. This was a pivotal moment for Weissmann, as it marked the first time he began to take into account the complex social, economic, and urban-planning challenges of working-class slums. Weissmann's initial experience in planning and his focus on the social dimensions of urban development led him to his first international assignment, commissioned by the Yugoslav Ministry of Social Policies and Public Health. Before heading to the CIAM congress in 1933, he embarked on his first trip to New York City to conduct a study of the living conditions of Yugoslav emigrants. Weissmann considered private ownership of land and the means of production as the main obstacles to slum clearance and the development of social mass housing. Supported by young, leftist

CIRPAC (CIAM's executive body) meeting in London, 1934: Le Corbusier, Ernest Weissmann, Josep Lluís Sert, and Wells Coates

architects from Spain, France, the United Kingdom, and the Netherlands during the fourth CIAM congress, Weissmann demanded the abolition of private ownership of land and the means of production and argued for the introduction of complex regional, instead of functional, urban planning. The requirements posed by the young architects were at the same time a response to Le Corbusier's and Sigfried Giedion's takeover of the CIAM leadership after the leftist German architects left for the USSR in 1930. In a world of growing political tensions, the new leadership headed towards the depoliticization of architecture and its articulation as an international style. As CIAM could not allow polarization between members needed for the preparation of congress materials, the young progressive architects were assigned to prepare the programme of the fifth congress. This congress, initially planned for 1935, focused on the relationship between cities and regions and on slum clearance.

Because of his engagement in preparing the fifth CIAM congress and the economic crises in Yugoslavia, Weissmann left his home country. In 1934, he lived and worked in London, collaborating with the MARS (Modern Architectural Research) Group – the UK's national group of CIAM. In February 1935, he moved to Paris again, the new centre of the CIAM's leftists and the city where the fifth congress would take place during the World Exhibition in 1937. Weissmann had the chance to live in France under a socialist government united to oppose growing fascism. He contributed to the activities of the Maison de la Culture's Architecture Secretariat, and he supported the Yugoslav volunteers who joined the Spanish Civil War and Communist Party of Yugoslavia leaders in exile. At the same time, he supervised the construction of the Yugoslav Pavilion at the Paris World Exhibition for a state that persecuted the communists. Due to political circumstances, the theme of the fifth CIAM congress was changed to "Housing and Leisure". At the congress, Weissmann and his like-minded colleagues reiterated their calls for coordinated efforts between housing programmes and economic and regional planning. They did so by summarizing their demands during a review of Le Corbusier's report "Solutions de principe" (basic solutions).[2] Their demands further included the adoption of the neighbourhood unit as the core element of city planning, wherein the residents are actively engaged in the development of their community. The fifth congress revealed yet again the failure of the younger architects and CIAM's leadership to meet in person and come to a consensus, which eventually led to the termination of further collaboration.

Despite the rupture withhin CIAM, Weissmann's activities in regional planning further intensified – and his theoretical stances were expounded in "Planification (Urbanisme) humaniste. Villes et campagnes" (Humanist urban planning. Cities and countryside).[3] His proposal was to use the region as a basic unit of integral planning, encompassing economic, social, and spatial aspects to achieve a more equitable distribution of resources and social well-being. This approach required mobilizing the latest technologies, industry, and local or state economies and administrations on a larger scale than hitherto. Weissmann had planned to present his ideas at the 15th International Congress of Architects in Washington, DC, and in early 1939 he travelled to the USA to oversee the execution of the Yugoslavian exhibition at the World Exhibition in New York.

2. *5e Congrès CIAM. Paris 1937. Logis et loisirs* (Boulogne-sur-Seine: L'Architecture d'Aujourd'hui, 1937).

3. Ernest Weissmann, "Planification (Urbanisme) humaniste'. Villes et campagne", New York, 1939. Ubu Gallery, New York, Marc Dessauce Collection. Ernest Weissmann Archive (further UBU-MDC-EWA, f. 1.6).

The Dymaxion Deployment Unit of Richard Buckminster Fuller, 1941, on which Ernest Weissmann collaborated

Post-war reconstruction

On the eve of the Second World War, Weissmann was a Jewish immigrant in New York. He tried to establish an architectural practice with Josep Lluís Sert and worked as a photographer and a cameraman for Kostich Colour Photos company. Once again, he collaborated with CIAM and he was part of New York's circle of left-wing technocrats, the American advocates of the New Objectivity, gathered around Richard Buckminster Fuller. Weissmann participated in the production of the prototype of Fuller's Dymaxion House, which he would largely document on film. His experience of industrial production served as a reference for employment on the US Board of Economic Warfare and the United Nations Relief and Rehabilitation Administration (UNRRA) in Washington between 1942 and 1947, where he participated in planning economic warfare and the reconstruction of industry and housing stock in post-war Europe and Asia. The goal was to make local communities self-sufficient, to give them knowledge and tools in order to help them develop their own plans for economic, social, and spatial development – both urban and rural. Weissmann continued to systematically implement and improve this method in his work. He described it in "Shelter, Relief, Rehabilitation of Housing in Rural and Urban Redevelopment", which was his contribution to CIAM's discussion of its members' role in the post-war reconstruction of Europe.[4]

4. Ernest Weissmann, "Shelter, Relief, Rehabilitation of Housing in Rural and Urban Redevelopment", 15 July 1944 (ETH, gta Archives, Zurich, f. 42-SG-2-228/230).

The board of consultants in charge of the construction of the United Nations headquarters building in New York, 1947: Le Corbusier second from the left, Ernest Weissmann second from the right

Weissmann advocated the participation of local architects, in addition to CIAM's professional support and partnership. For him, the only possible theme of the first post-war CIAM congress was "New Standard of Values for Community Development".[5] That same year, Weissmann renewed his collaboration with Le Corbusier by taking part in the design for the United Nations headquarters building in New York.

At UNRRA, Weissmann mastered skills crucial for his future line of work – planning, negotiating, and implementing international projects and developmental policies. In 1947, he took on a managerial position as a director of the Industry and Materials Division of the UN Economic Commission for Europe in Geneva. Once again, his professional task was to deliver a report on the housing situation in post-war Europe and establish the industry and inter-European collaboration required. In 1951, returning to the US, Weissmann became a director of the Housing and Town and Country Planning Section and in 1956 an assistant director of the Housing, Building and Planning Unit, both at the UN Department of Economic and Social Affairs in New York. In a period of intensive decolonization, Cold War, and the "Red Scare", the 47-year-old Weissmann was finally given the chance to implement his vision of planned economic, social, and spatial development as part of the UN's actions and programmes.

5. Ernest Weissmann, "Opinion on the program of the Sixth CIAM Congress", 13 May 1947 (UBU-MDC-EWA, f. 1.5).

The United Nations: Housing, Building, and Planning

Weissmann's priority at the UN Department of Economic and Social Affairs was "to handle housing problems" in the less-developed countries of the Middle East, Asia, Latin America, and Africa – the acute housing crisis caused by wartime destruction, demographic "bombs", and great migrations from rural to urban areas. Although "the crisis [was] complex" and "deeply rooted in world economic and world trade patterns",[6] Weissmann still believed "that our century may be remembered in future centuries not as an age of political conflicts or technical invention, but as an age in which society dared to think of the welfare of the whole human race as a practicable objective".[7]

Cover of "Housing and Town and Country Planning Bulletin" no. 6, 1952, published by the Housing and Town and Country Planning Section of the Department of Social Affairs headed by Ernest Weissmann

With a small team of experts and modest financial resources, Weissmann worked diligently on the "building up of an infrastructure of knowledge, skills and understanding required to produce a viable community development policy and program in the developing countries" that was based on economic, regional, and spatial planning.[8] Weissmann established a programme of action, and thorough analytical and systematic theoretical and practical work in the field of housing and planning. Before his arrival, the UN's work on housing and planning had been limited to the collection and exchange of information, and studies of a more general character. A series of studies and joint pilot projects by the UN and national governments in specific fields were launched – regional, rural, and metropolitan planning; low-cost housing; community improvements; housing and building research; the education of professional staff; the financing and implementation of housing-construction programmes that value the contributions of housing cooperatives and a self-help approach. The studies and projects were used to define methods and techniques that might assist governments to initiate "massive and sustained" national action using their own resources. Weissmann presented the results of accomplished work regularly in the UN *Housing and Town and Country Planning Bulletin* in the form of thematic issues.

6. Ernest Weissmann, "The Role of the UN in Urban Research and Planning", in: Leo F. Schnore and Henry Fagin (eds), *Urban Research and Policy Planning* (Beverly Hills, CA: Sage Publications, 1967), Vol. I, 553–581, at 556.

7. Weissmann, "The Role of the UN", 558.

8. Weissmann, "The Role of the UN", 560.

Members of the working group for the Skopje reconstruction master plan around a competition model, with Weissmann (at middle-right with glasses), 1965

The main role in mediating knowledge was given to the UN's experts, partly recruited within CIAM members, and newly established institutions – regional centres and schools for housing, community, regional, and rural planning in Latin America, Asia, and Africa. Collaborations and the exchange of knowledge with other international organizations and UN agencies working in the field of housing, universities, and foundations were conducted through conferences and international regional seminars. Although Weissmann's efforts to establish a fruitful collaboration with CIAM at the occasion of the eighth Congress in Hoddesdon in 1951 did not meet with approval, he successfully collaborated with Team 10 members on several occasions.

The global housing crisis, the unplanned spread of cities, and the excessive exploitation of natural sources, often emphasized by Weissmann, were causes for concerted international action in the early 1960s. The United Nations introduced the UN Development Decade and UN Development Programme, intended to provide help in the national planning of economic and social growth, housing-construction development, urban renewal, slum clearance, and rural development. Weissmann was a member of a newly established committee responsible for the programme of Housing, Building and Planning of the UN Development Decade, which was presented to the General Assembly in 1964. The programme was a long-awaited opportunity to bring to the fore the concept of "balanced development".

The usually divided fields of housing and city planning – a place where social and economic programmes meet – became part of national development programmes and regional planning. The region was still the basic planning unit, which Weissmann considered to be appropriate for both developed and underdeveloped countries.

Together with his associates, Weissmann organized a series of events (conferences, seminars, workshops, professional trips, regional meetings), and the projects of the UN and national governments which were still the main testing platform for implementing and expanding knowledge. Over a span of several years (1962–1965), 30 joint projects in housing, community facilities, and urban development were executed. The reconstruction of Skopje after the devastating earthquake in 1963 and the low-cost housing project in Previ, Lima are representative examples of the interdisciplinary, international, professional, and scientific collaboration advocated by Weissmann. He retired from his position as director of the UN Centre for Housing, Building and Planning in 1966.

As a senior advisor, following the new set of priorities, Weissmann continued to work on education projects tailored for the new generations of professionals in the field of regional development planning trained to take their role in economic and social development. The first UN Centre for Regional Development (UNCRD) was founded in Nagoya in Japan. Weissmann collaborated with the centre for several years on the issues of metropolitan region planning. He worked on founding similar centres in Latin America, Africa, and Europe – and participated in the UN's joint projects in the USSR, Pakistan, and Yugoslavia. The next important phase of the UN's activities was the launching of the UN Environment Programme (UNEP) in 1972, whose goal was to guide and coordinate environmental activities within the UN system. Weissmann was a senior consultant for the Action and Training Programmes in Human Settlements. He helped organize Habitat I – the first conference of the United Nations on human settlements, sustainable development, and the environment in Vancouver in 1976. The Habitat Charter was the fulfilment of his efforts, which had been conceived as early as the 1930s – an understanding of the "crucial role of settlements for the 3 functions (econom. loc., soc. jus., env. bal.) [local economy, social justice, environmental balance]".[9] However, at the end of his career and life, in the mid-1980s, Weissmann concluded, "Conference's recommendations for action were never really taken down to the working level" within the UN.[10] Once again, despite his commitment and outstanding efforts, he became a collateral victim due to the system's inertia. Luckily, Weissmann, who was a stubborn and "pragmatic idealist", had always had the strength to overcome such professional challenges.[11] His work from 1941 onwards, which spans across almost all continents, has yet to be adequately researched.

9. Ernest Weissmann, "Professional Life", Gordon Weissmann Archive, Boston, MA, 3.

10. Weissmann, "Professional Life", 3.

11. Anon., "Homage to Enci: A Practical Idealist in the UN Secretariat", Teodorović family archive, Zagreb.

35, rue de Sèvres
A day in the life,
summer 1929

During an afternoon in 1929, Ernest Weissmann and his colleagues film themselves and their masters at work at the Atelier Le Corbusier and Pierre Jeanneret. The filmed sequences offer a unique and intimate visual witness of collaborators' scarcely gathered memories of their days at 35, rue de Sèvres in interviews or biographies. These memories act as a confirmation of what Weissmann and his friends capture that day in the Atelier: a working meeting between Le Corbusier and Pierre Jeanneret; the follow-up by Pierre Jeanneret of the projects the collaborators are working on; and, in between, some "lost" moments of enjoyment amongst friends.

The film reels filmed inside the Atelier were too dark to be viewed and were probably never seen by Weissmann or his friends. Thanks to the recent frame-by-frame digitalization, people and situations could be perceived and identified. The film sequence starts by filming the exterior of the Atelier. A big tree in the inner court of the ancient cloister at 35, rue de Sèvres is filmed from top to bottom, unveiling at the same time the façades of the cloister wing where the Atelier had moved in five years before, in July 1924. The children of the caretaker pose as if they were to be photographed, ignoring the new modalities of capturing. The sequences filmed in the Atelier do not reveal the workplace itself, a long high-ceilinged corridor more than 40 m long and only 3.5 m wide on the first floor, but focus on the activities that were taking place. Kunio Maekawa is filmed next to the window, to let a maximum of light enter the camera. Pierre Jeanneret is captured at several moments: alone, with collaborators, and with Le Corbusier. Two sequences show Weissmann himself, the first while he's putting on his lab coat, against the background of a nearly empty Atelier – the only shot that enables us to grasp a view into the depth of the long room, with the drawing tables lined up one after the other. The second shows Weissmann, standing, with Pierre Jeanneret explaining a drawing to him – both in the light of the open window. One could question who took the camera over from him: was it one of the other collaborators, Maekawa or Norman Rice, who were certainly present that afternoon as they are captured in other sequences; would it have been Pierre Jeanneret, himself a fervent photographer and fan of new techniques; or did Le Corbusier take the occasion to experiment with this new machine, some years before borrowing a camera himself for photographing and filming?[1] The question remains unanswered, but the overall answer shown in these images is the excitement of the new technology of filming, of filming each other, and of being filmed.

The filmed interior sequences are quite short, jumping from one subject to another, almost like moving photographs. Maybe this is one of the first times Weissmann used his new camera, or maybe it is due to the act of filming by his friends. These sequences come closest to the idea of amateur filming: making photographs that move. From all the filming he did over the years, these amateur reels could be categorized on the one hand as leisure – by filming trips, friends, and lost moments – and on the other hand as remembering the start of his professional life – filming buildings, constructions, etc. Filming at the Atelier can be seen as the ultimate fusion of those two categories, combining here informal moments

1. Tim Benton, *LC Foto: Le Corbusier: Secret Photographer* (Zurich: Lars Müller, 2013).

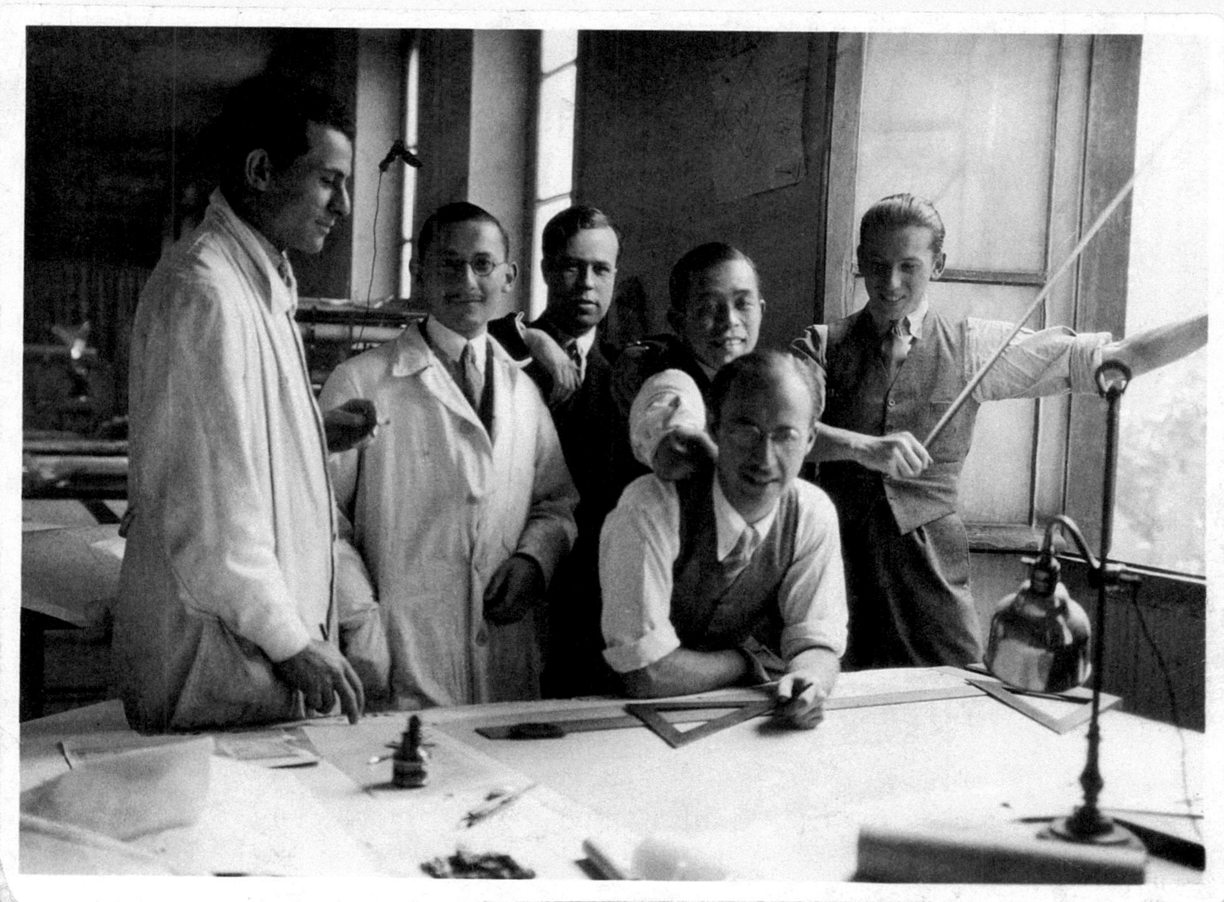

The collaborators at the Atelier in October 1929, Eugene Rosenberg, another Czechoslovak collaborator, and the "close" gang: Josep Lluís Sert, Kunio Maekawa, Norman Rice at the drawing table, and Ernest Weissmann

with his friends at work, as well as teasing his masters at work by recording them. Filming friends at work, motivated by the occasion to work at one the most famous avant-garde architect's offices of that time – but, that day, also excited by the filming – shows perfectly how much working at the Atelier was a complete experience for Weissmann and the other collaborators, with whom he would stay in contact for the rest of his life, both for professional occasions as well as for the friendship on which these occasions were based. The excitement of working together set the atmosphere in the Atelier. The energy, enthusiasm, and intensity of working at the Atelier was testified to by Le Corbusier in the second volume of the *Œuvre complète 1929-1934*:

> To tell the truth, a lot of hard work was done. It was the help of young people that made it possible. Until 1927, there were two of us: Pierre Jeanneret and me. From then on, we found ourselves enlarged by an ever-changing and renewed volume of youthful energy and dedication. The collaboration of young people, who came from all over the world with full confidence and an intense desire to learn, brought together in our workshop powers of work which, at certain times, became extraordinary, and it was not under the sign of weariness or boredom that this work was undertaken and carried out, but under the sign of love. An intense love of the truth.[2]

2. Boesiger, Willy and Oscar Stonorov, eds. *Le Corbusier et Pierre Jeanneret. Œuvre complète 1929-1934*. (Zurich: Girsberger, 1935), 19.

Photomontage of the many collaborators at the Atelier Le Corbusier at the end of the 1940s

The longest sequence is dedicated to a working meeting between Le Corbusier and Pierre Jeanneret. Limited lighting from a lamp leaving the surroundings dark make it very intimate to look at. The filmed sequence of the meeting starts in a very relaxed atmosphere, a simple pendant lamp above the desk is waltzing from one side to another, as is the camera. The laughing faces of Le Corbusier and Pierre Jeanneret appear and disappear by the movements of the lamp and the camera, the event of bringing a camera in the Atelier and filming creates clearly joyful fuss during work time. The masters are filmed from all sides and distances: one moment, the two protagonists leaning over a plan emphasizes the impression of participating in a common but hidden moment. Suddenly, their faces turn towards the camera, they smile, they know they are being filmed. In the darkness behind, a collaborator, probably Rice, is passing back and forth. The camera offers a glimpse of the desk, and the stack of paperwork and letters on it. The architects did not have a personal office, like the "box" Le Corbusier would realize in the 1950s, nor a secretary – and paperwork and letters often passed through the hands of the collaborators before it was seen by the masters, as Charlotte Perriand witnessed.[3]

During these years, the configuration of the Atelier reveals organization but with a certain sense of chaos. Le Corbusier split his day into two distinctive parts: during the morning, he worked from home on what he called his personal "patient

3. Hélène Cauquil and Marc Bedarida, "Le Corbusier. L'Atelier 35 rue de Sèvres", *Bulletin d'information architecturale de l'Institut Français d'Architecture*, supplement to no. 114, Summer 1987, 11.

research": writing, painting, but also more collective work by working on the conceptional phase of projects; the afternoon was dedicated to the collaborative and professional work at the Atelier. From the beginning of the 1950s, he would invert this order due to his age, but the principle of the day split day into a personal and a collaborative part would persist during his whole life. These "five hours, every day" in the afternoon were then taken to check and answer letters; to discuss projects with Pierre Jeanneret; and, as witnessed by Charlotte Perriand, "at the end of the day Le Corbusier would come by and examine each project carefully. What an opportunity for all of us!"[4] Norman Rice recalls his memories of the extraordinary period at the Atelier: "Le Corbusier was there nearly every day – always there was Pierre Jeanneret, cousin and partner – a wonderful time, working, discussing, working, arguing, always about architecture, with him, between ourselves, first it was purgative, then stimulant, then nutriment, often ambrosia – and we were in Paris!"[5]

The portrayal of Pierre Jeanneret by Weissmann – who would keep in close contact with Pierre Jeanneret after leaving Paris – is crucial in understanding his position in the Atelier. Leading the office with his cousin Le Corbusier and being ten years his junior places him in between the collaborators, with whom there was often less age difference, and Le Corbusier, and offers him often a confidentiality role. This confidentiality can be grasped by the way he is being filmed that day by the collaborators: first as one of the two masters, in discussion during their meeting; afterwards as a patient and confidential instructor, taking the time to explain architectural solutions to the collaborators; and as a relaxed workmate, laughing and smoking. His presence amongst the collaborators, forming the link between what has been discussed with Le Corbusier and the practical output that needed to be done, visualizes here the memories of Charlotte Perriand about the atmosphere between the collaborators and with the bosses in the Atelier: "Jeanneret followed all the details of the execution with us. He himself researched and drew the smallest details endlessly".[6]

Today, only a few other images testify to the occupation of the long cloister corridor, with the positions of the drawing tables, the barely functioning stove in the middle, the light bulbs hanging from the ceiling, and the walls gradually more covered by project plans. Some photographs bear witness to the working rhythm, and especially capture the festive moments after sleepless nights for handing over plans. On one occasion, Le Corbusier and Pierre Jeanneret open the Atelier to the public in the film *Les Mains de Paris* (1934), which shows a discussion with the masters and the collaborators around some projects of that moment: a model of the Palace of the Soviets project, a model of the agricultural reorganization project, and plans of the Pavillon Suisse. None of the collaborators present at the time of Weissmann witnessed this event, as by then they had all flown out over the world – their places taken by a new generation of enthusiastic young architects.

Le Corbusier looking at a model, photographed by Weissmann; in the background are the plans of the Mundaneum.

4. Cauquil and Bedarida, "Le Corbusier. L'Atelier 35 rue de Sèvres", 11.

5. Norman Rice, "I remember 35 rue de Sèvres", *PSA News*, May 1981, 6.

6. Cauquil and Bedarida, "Le Corbusier. L'Atelier 35 rue de Sèvres", 11.

Le Corbusier, Pierre Jeanneret, and their collaborators in 1934 at the Atelier, presenting the model of the Palace of the Soviets in the film *Les Mains de Paris* of Alexander Alexander (1934)

Le Corbusier, 1964, in the Atelier with his collaborators, during the filming for Gilbert Prouteau's never-released documentary on Le Corbusier, the last film on the architect

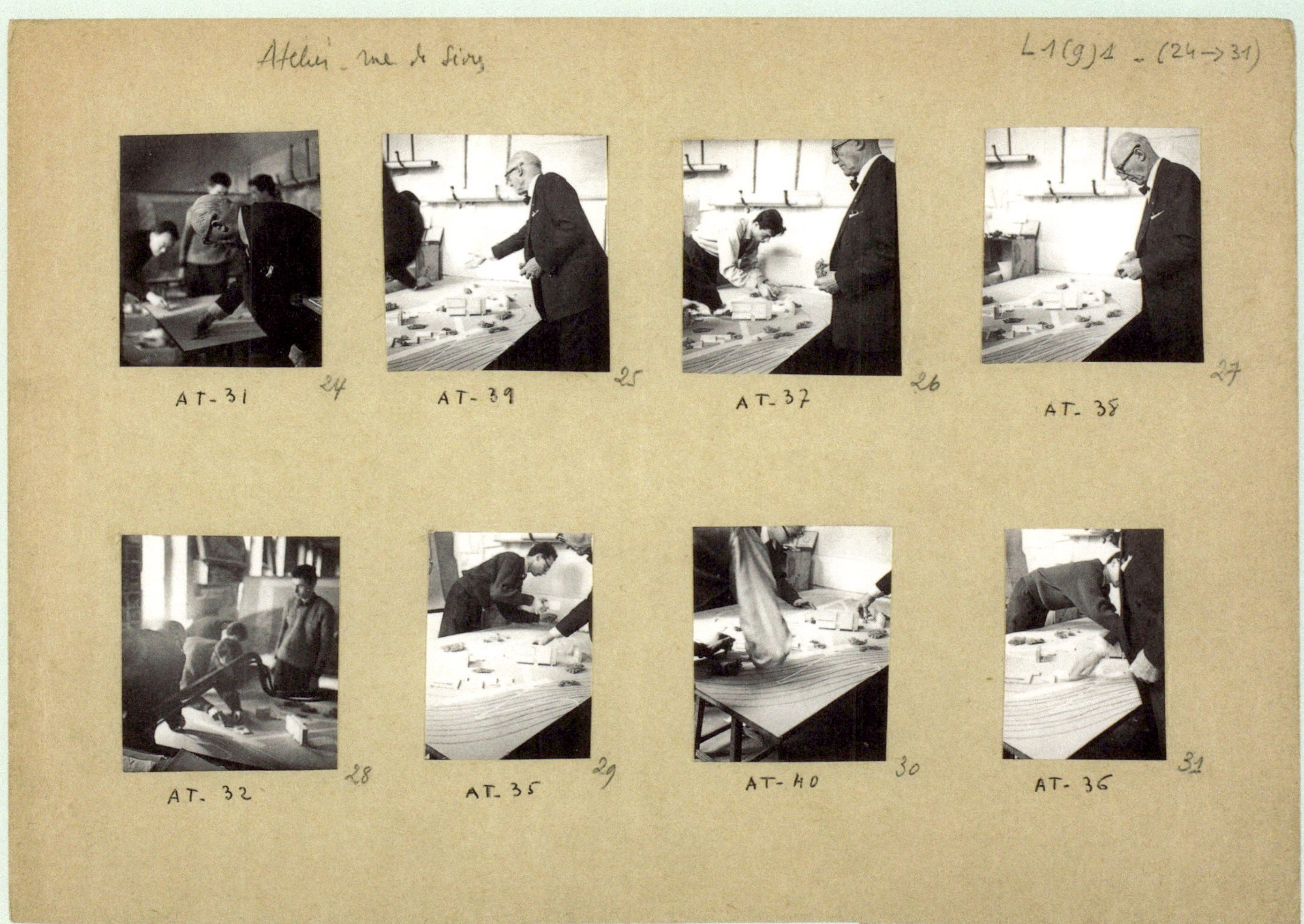

Contact sheet of a photographic series that Lucien Hervé realized of a meeting between Le Corbusier and some collaborators at the Atelier

After the Second World War, when Le Corbusier reopened the Atelier for his own office, until his death in 1965, pictures of the collaborators at work in the Atelier are more common, and some photographic coverage was done for lifestyle magazines – for example, by Willy Rizzo in 1953 for *Paris Match* and René Burri in 1959.[7] Besides the voyeuristic aspect offered by the popular press, the Atelier was also used on some occasions as the background for film or television interviews, with Le Corbusier taking an official representative function – for example, the biographical documentary on Le Corbusier that the French poet Gilbert Prouteau directed just before the death of the architect, or the television documentary *Paris à sauver, Paris à reconstruire* of 1960 by Max-Pol Fouchet, where André Wogenscky takes the floor instead of Le Corbusier. But Le Corbusier would also more and more refuse visits to the Atelier, seen as bothering him and preventing the collaborators from working. It is telling that, for photoshoots as well as documentaries for television and film, he would prefer to open up the so-called private sphere of the home, his apartment at rue Nungesser-et-Coli, rather than his workplace of forty years standing.

7. René Burri and Arthur Rüegg, *Le Corbusier: Photographs by René Burri/ Magnum: Moments in the Life of a Great Architect* (Basel: Birkhäuser Verlag, 1999).

Children at the conciergerie at 35, rue de Sèvres,
preparing to pose as for a photograph

The inner courtyard of 35, rue de Sèvres, with the wing of the ancient cloister building where the Atelier was housed

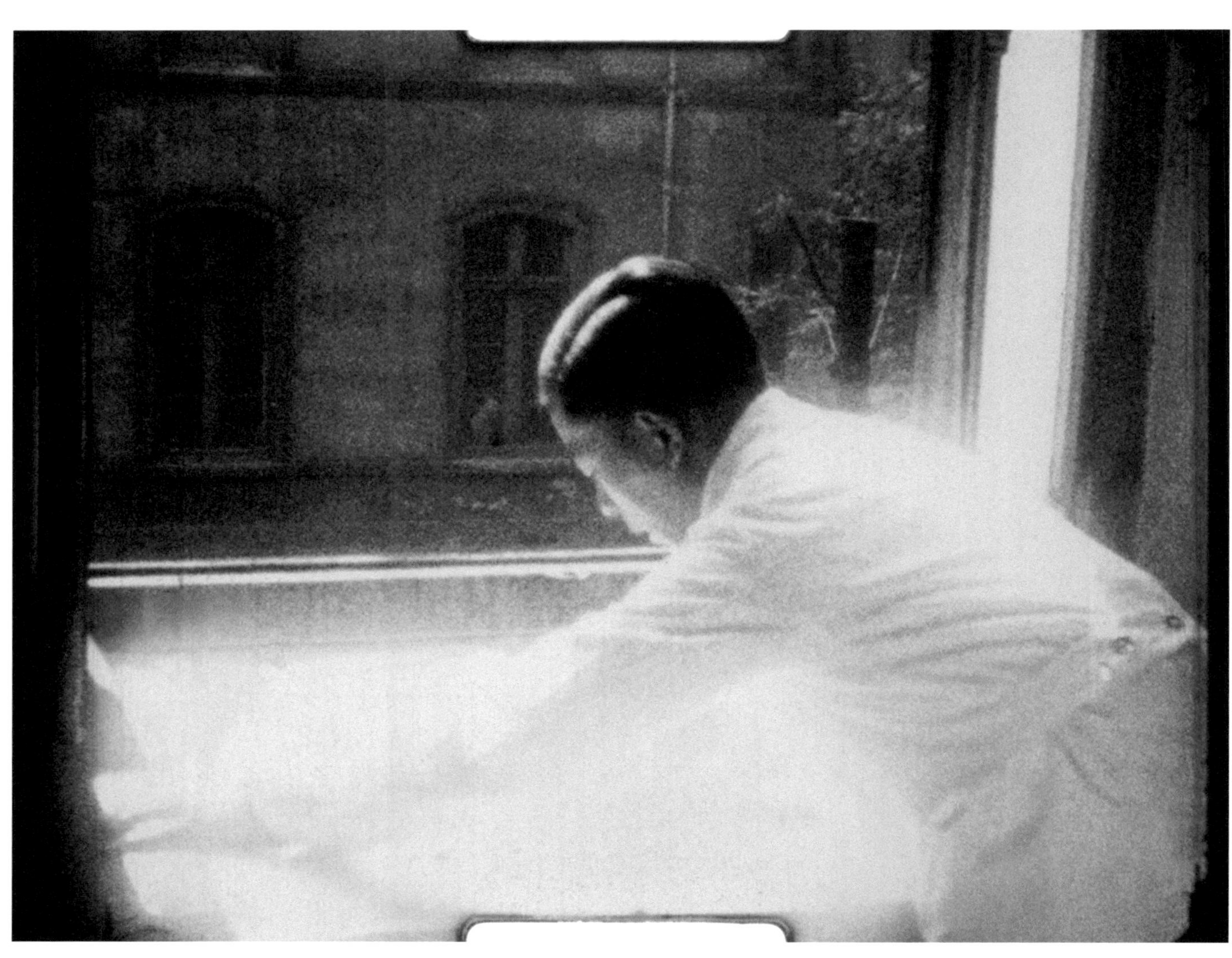

Kunio Maekawa in his lab coat with a plan, before the open window of the Atelier

Pierre Jeanneret in total concentration, drawing on a plan

Close-up portraits of Le Corbusier and Pierre Jeanneret in deep concentration, discussing projects and drawing on plans

A working meeting between Le Corbusier and Pierre Jeanneret is captured from a certain distance. The masters stand bowed over the table, discussing projects and plans. Le Corbusier is looking up; they know they are being filmed.

Ernest Weissmann at the window of the Atelier putting on his lab coat; the long, narrow space of the Atelier seems dark and empty

Orders are given by Pierre Jeanneret to the collaborators after the meeting between the masters. Here, he explains the plan that Ernest Weissmann, pictured in his lab coat, must draw.

Le Corbusier, smoking a cigarette, at the office table behind a stack of paperwork

Pierre Jeanneret seated before the open window of the Atelier, smoking a cigarette while drawing and explaining

2

A journey by aeroplane, June 1929

On the morning of 6 June 1929, Le Corbusier takes a Farman Goliath aeroplane from Le Bourget to Berlin, from where he will continue his trip by train to Moscow to arrange the start of the execution of the Centrosoyus project. The departure is an exhausting event, as it is the first time Le Corbusier will have travelled by plane. Seeing, and especially taking, a plane was not an everyday affair, as the filming witnesses – and on top of that, it would be in the iconic Farman Goliath, which Le Corbusier had already publicized in 1923 in *Vers une architecture*! Ernest Weissmann films the whole event from the moment both architects head off from Paris to the Le Bourget airport until the take-off of the plane. The filmed images convey not only excitement about the forthcoming execution of the Atelier's first large project but also a fascination with the ability to cross distant borders, and interest in the aeroplane as a solution to the new questions of the machine age.

The trip to Moscow is Le Corbusier's second visit to the USSR, after his first trip in October of the previous year. Le Corbusier would return to Moscow for a third and last visit the following year, in March 1930, visiting the Centrosoyus building site. The first and longest trip, in 1928, was intended to present the competition project in person, and his visit took on a great public and media dimension as Le Corbusier took advantage of his venue to give lectures, to meet personalities – of which the meeting with film director Sergei Eisenstein is certainly still the most widely known today – to discover Moscow's architecture, and to build up new contacts. The second trip was much shorter, with barely three days in Moscow, and was organized in a hurry in order to prepare the execution of the Centrosoyus project, with a few work sessions "where I made my ideas triumph".[7] The contract had in fact been signed only a week before, on 1 June 1929, which gave him little time to organize the journey. However, this haste was an opportunity to try out other means of transport, which shortened the journey time: the plane. Le Corbusier recalls, in *Aircraft* in 1935, his journey and his fascination for this international network, its equipment, and its punctuality:

> In [1928], before setting out for Moscow, I thought I would shorten the journey by taking an airplane. I discovered the airports at Le Bourget, Cologne, and Berlin. I perceived that people by dint of faith and determination had little by little, higgledy-piggledy, equipped hangars, instruments, buildings, and staff. And that the airports were stations like railway stations. One set off at a given time and, lo! one arrived with chronometric exactitude.[8]

The journey to Moscow was made in several stages. Le Corbusier took a first flight from Le Bourget to Cologne, a journey that lasted less than three hours; "this is safety itself",[9] he noted to his mother. After the stopover the flight continued to Berlin, where he arrived in the afternoon at 4 pm. The arrival in Moscow was scheduled for 24 hours later the next day, by train. Le Corbusier's smiling face before departure, filmed by Weissmann, conceals his nervousness about taking off – knowing the risks of taking a plane and suffering from severe seasickness.

7. Letter from Le Corbusier to Jean Herbette, Ambassador of France in Moscow, 25 June 1929 (FLC, H2-9-99).

8. Le Corbusier, *Aircraft*, "The New Vision" series (London–New York: The Studio, 1935), 10. Le Corbusier errs here – mentioning 1928 (that journey was done by train).

9. Postcard from Le Corbusier to his mother from Cologne, 6 June 1929 (FLC, R2-1-421).

Postcard of an aerial view of Cologne from Le Corbusier to his mother when he arrived at the airport in Cologne, in which he reports on his first experience in a plane

The postcards he sent to his wife, Yvonne, and his mother on his arrival in Cologne leave no doubt about that:

> I'm having lunch. Disobliged at ten o'clock. Slept afterwards. Woke up bewildered, in a neat and tidy airport. Staggered on my legs. Can't find my words in German: can't hear anything! I realize that my ears are clogged with cotton. The earth seen from above makes me think. As for the plane, it is safety, regularity, truth.[10]

This first experience let Le Corbusier discover a new, modern network – the air network – installed throughout the densely built-up territories of Europe, with airlines and a whole new infrastructure. It offered the architect reflection on a new era for network and speed, as would be crystallized some ten years later in *Sur les 4 routes*. The entire airport setting, as well as the heading off from Paris, filmed by Weissmann, contributes to this experience. The Le Bourget airport – at the time the only civil airport in Paris, and to remain so for a further ten years – was booming, and in 1929 had more than 45,000 passengers, which meant more than ten planes

The Lossier hangars, which were built in 1927 to house the Farman aeroplanes at Le Bourget. The various buildings of the airport were discussed and illustrated in *La Construction Moderne* the same year, and published as postcards.

10. Postcards from Le Corbusier to his mother and to Yvonne Gallis (FLC, R2-1-42).

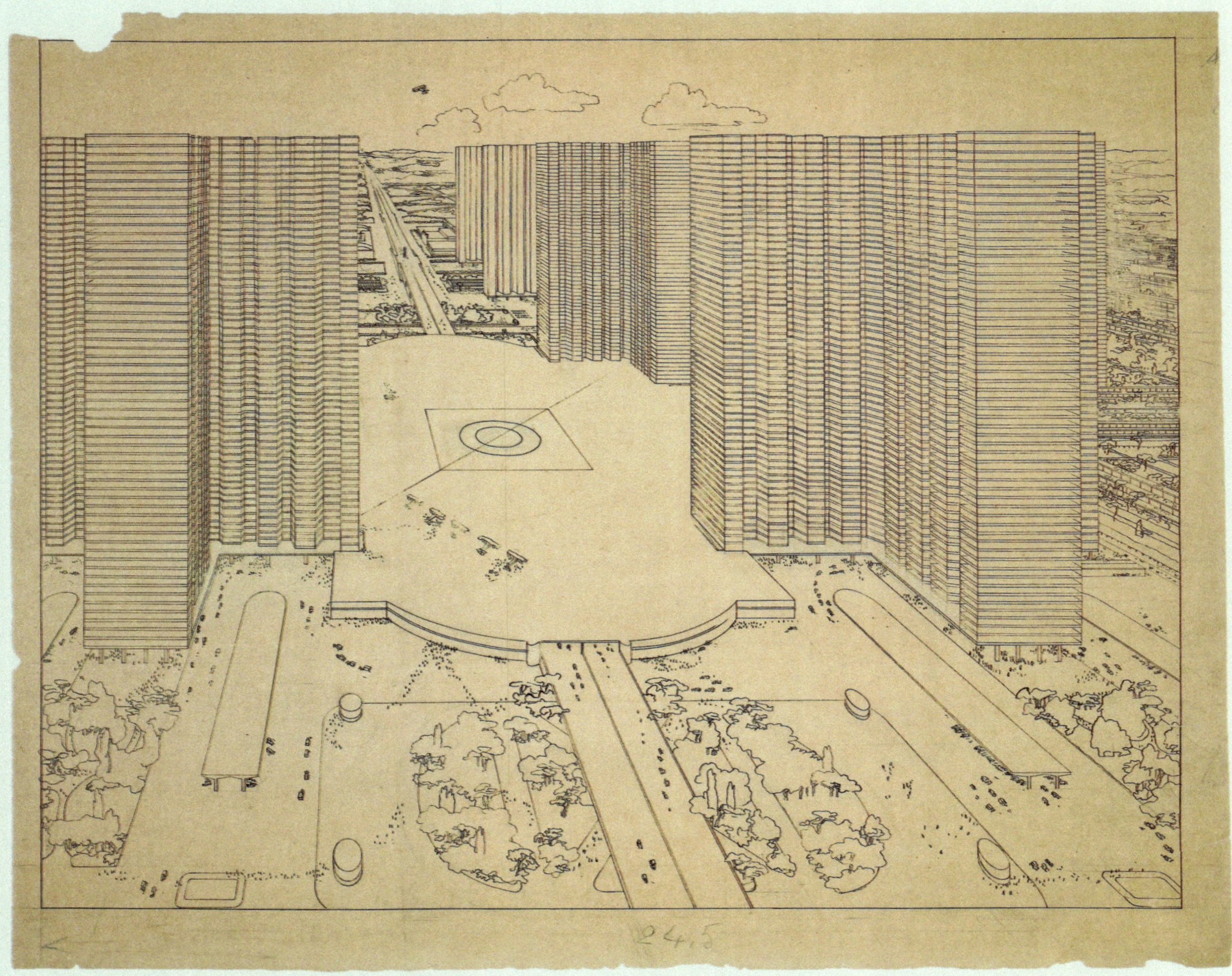

This perspective of the Contemporary City of 3 Million Inhabitants of 1922 shows the airport strip in the middle of the city, between the towers. For the concretization of the Paris project of 1925, the Plan Voisin, Le Corbusier contacted both the automobile and aircraft industries looking for sponsorship.

a day. We are still a long way from Georges Labro's new terminal buildings, whose competition was launched in 1935 to compete with the airports of London and Berlin – both major destinations from Le Bourget. The main buildings of the airport seen in the images are the hangars built by engineer Henry Lossier in 1921–1922, with reinforced-concrete vaults, each capable of housing six Farman aircraft. Adjacent to the hangars are the premises that housed, among others, the offices of the airlines, from where we see Le Corbusier coming out, with a big smile, putting his wallet back in his coat. Neither Weissmann nor his masters paid much attention to the architecture of the hangars, which was an exemplary engineering project with its thin concrete walls. The architecture is in the background; the focus is on these incredible flying machines. Behind the hangars, there is still-undeveloped land – and the urbanization of the Aviation district, with the Cité 212 and the Cité Pont-Yblon by Germain Dorel, would only take place a few years later. Nonetheless, in contrast to his admiration for the vastness of the virgin, unbuilt land outside of Paris and the distant horizons of travel that one can perceive in the film stills, Le Corbusier is also very critical about the remote position of Le Bourget: "the exile of the sordid suburbs"[11] of Paris. The time gained by travelling by air is, for Le Corbusier, annihilated by the position of the airport outside the city, lacking a decent route, and its disconnection from the

11. Le Corbusier, *Sur les 4 routes* (Paris: Gallimard, 1941), 120.

DES YEUX QUI NE VOIENT PAS... 99

FARMAN.

other networks.[12] It evokes the importance for Le Corbusier of situating the airports in the very centre of his urban-design projects – as seen in the Plan for a City of 3 Million Inhabitants and the Plan Voisin, but also in the urban-design project for the Left Bank of Antwerp of 1933, where Le Corbusier designed an airport in the new city centre even though the city of Antwerp had, only two years earlier, inaugurated its new airport in the suburbs of Deurne.

While Weissmann is filming at the Bourget airport, he is not only covering the exceptionality of his master's trip by following Le Corbusier from the check-in until his climbing on board the plane, while he is admiring the come-and-go of aeroplanes and discussing with the pilot. Weissmann also uses his camera to capture the mechanics of the aeroplane, the span of the wings, the motors, the landing system. By the close attention he is giving to details of the plane, and also how Le Corbusier pays attention to them, it becomes clear how this first close encounter with a plane was important and decisive for all of them. It recalls the importance Le Corbusier had already placed on the aeroplane from his first publication onwards: *Vers une architecture*, published in 1923, where photographs of aeroplanes – many of them are images of Farman planes – are abundantly used as the illustration of a clear response to a clear need. Le Corbusier carefully kept in his archives the brochures, photographs, and other promotional material of the Farman industry that he used for the publication. In the chapter "Eyes which do not see", alongside the attention devoted to cars and ocean liners, Le Corbusier discusses over 20 pages the lessons to be learned by architecture from the plane. Le Corbusier refers to planes as a logical creation of engineers, the result of reasoning:

The Farman planes are abundantly shown in Le Corbusier's first publication, *Vers une architecture*. Here, a picture of a Farman Goliath aircraft as a clear message of a design that responds to its needs

> the lesson of the plane is not so much in the forms created, and, first, one must learn not to see in a plane a bird or a dragonfly, but a machine to fly; the lesson of the plane is in the logic that presided over the statement of the problem and that leads to the success of its realization. When a problem is posed, in our time it inevitably finds its solution. The problem of the house is not posed.[13]

12. Le Corbusier, *Précisions sur un état présent de l'architecture et de l'urbanisme* (Paris: Les Éditions G. Crès & Cie, 1930), 255.

13. Le Corbusier, *Vers une architecture*, Collection de "L'Esprit Nouveau" (Paris: Les Éditions G. Crès & Cie, 1923), 85.

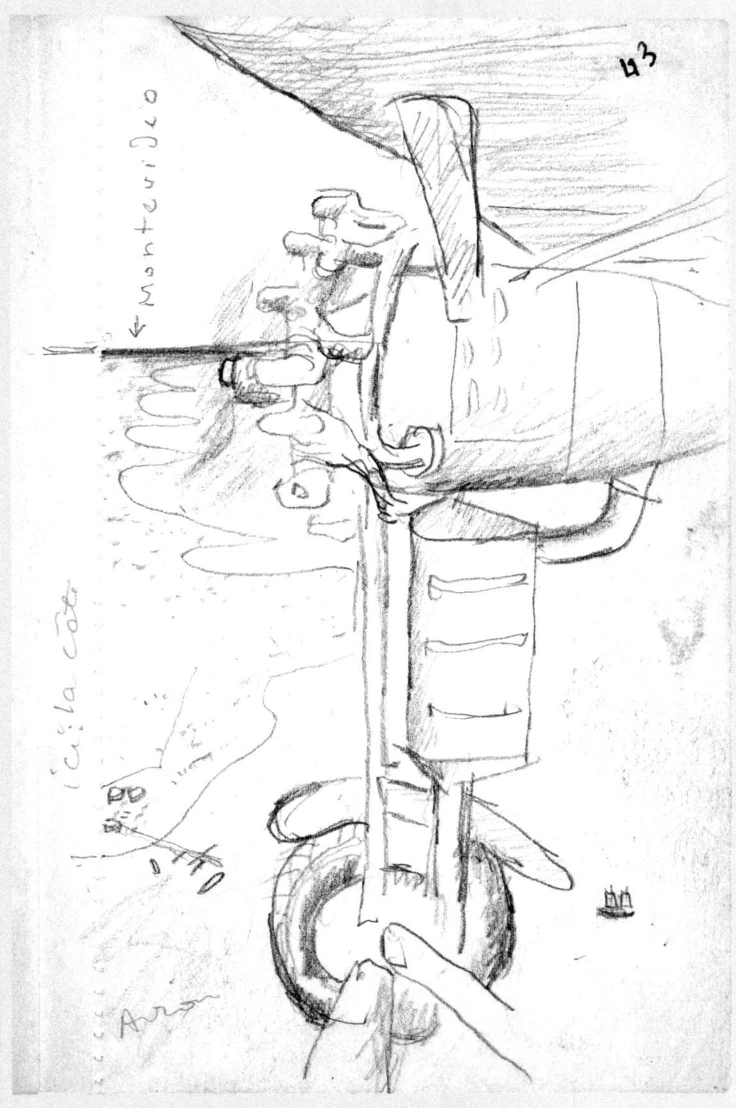

Le Corbusier, who here draws the motor and landing system of the plane he took at the end of 1929 in Montevideo, shares Ernest Weissmann's curiosity about the mechanics of the aircraft.

It is this admiration for rational and pure creation that he also transmits to Ernest Weissmann. The latter, always interested in the technicality of objects, took the time to film the plane to capture the essential idea: the machine's solution to the question of flying. One can perceive his admiration for the technology of aeroplanes, as Weissmann observes with his camera all the mechanics and construction. Le Corbusier would also capture in drawings the technicality of motor and landing gear when taking another aeroplane a few months later in Montevideo, recalling the excitement of the first encounter at Le Bourget with Weissmann. When, in 1935, *Aircraft* was published as the first book in the series "The New Vision", the publisher called on Le Corbusier for that very reason: to show how he, as a contemporary "designer", was influenced by the industrial world and particularly by the objects of the aircraft. Several influences for Le Corbusier are expressed here – the mechanics, the efficiency of the timetable, and the view of the sky among them.

The aeroplane Le Corbusier flew with had been developed as a bomber. Le Corbusier refers in *Vers une architecture* to the iconic Farman F.60 Goliath, and how "[w]ar as insatiable client" had pushed the development of the bomber plane. From 1919 until the end of the 1920s, these bombers were transformed into commercial aircraft that could carry passengers. When Le Corbusier took the F-FARI plane, it had already undergone a second transformation and could by then carry up to twelve people – two pilots and ten passengers – no longer in the light rattan seats shown in the promotional brochure he obtained but in more comfortable leather seats. The new decade brought new, larger, and more powerful aircraft models – and Le Corbusier's trip in a Farman Goliath was therefore also an image of an era of early commercial flight that was coming to an end. In the years that followed, the number of passengers on commercial flights would rise dramatically – with technical and capacity advances in aircraft responding to this growth. Some photographs taken of Le Corbusier in an aeroplane in 1935 flying from Chicago to New York, just five years after his trip in a Farman Goliath, show a travel environment that was much more advanced in terms of technology and comfort than the 1929 trip.

alliage d'acier spécialement traité à chaud.

Fuselage en tubes d'acier; recouvrement en toile. Freins à action indépendante ou simultanée sur les roues.

gure (plan supérieur), $24^{m},38$ et (inférieur), $20^{m},1$; longueur $17^{m},06$; hauteur, $3^{m},85$. Surface $113^{m2},3$. Poids total en vol, 6573^{kg}. Charge au mètre carré, $58^{kg},1$; au HP, 5^{kg}.

Cabine et installations motrices du trimoteur de transport BOEING

Une adaptation nouvelle du "Goliath" de transport

Destiné aux lignes roumaines, ce nouveau "*Goliath*" est équipé de deux *Armstrong-Siddeley* "*Jaguar*" 365 HP. Pour la première fois dans ce type classique, les cintres des cadres remplacent les barres de compression. Extension des glaces ouvrantes à toutes les baies; fenêtres vitrées dans le plafond; double commande en conduite intérieure. Poids à vide, équipé, 3300^{kg}; combustible suffisant pour 700^{km}, 820^{kg}; charge payante, 1200^{kg}.

Ci-dessous, poste de pilotage et cabine. *Ci-dessus, aspect latéral du fuselage.*

Inside view of the Farman Goliath, modernized at the beginning of 1929, as published in *L'Aéronoautique* in January 1929

Le Corbusier pictured in a plane from Chicago to New York, in 1935, on Thanksgiving. By this time, American monoplanes were already offering much greater levels of comfort than the European biplanes of some years earlier.

Double interior page 30-31 of the 1935 publication *Aircraft*, by Le Corbusier, giving his vision of the importance and challenges for aeroplanes

Besides the experience of the air network, Le Corbusier's first air trip above the densely built-up territories of Europe consolidated the urban-design lessons the bird's-eye view from a plane offers: "The earth seen from above makes me think", as he reflects to his future wife, Yvonne, and his mother. Only a few months later, he would experience the earth seen from the air above another continent. During his stay in Buenos Aires and Rio de Janeiro in October and November that year, he enjoyed three other trips by aeroplane, which deeply impressed him about the natural vastness of the South American landscape. Besides a trip in a hydroplane, and one in a small plane with only the pilot and him flying over Rio, he was able to join the inaugural trip of 1000 km by the "Compagnie Sud-Américaine de Navigation Aérienne", from Buenos Aires to Asunción in Paraguay in a Latécoère plane, in the company of Jean Mermoz and Antoine de Saint-Exupéry – an experience he largely covered in *Précisions*, a publication that was the result of that long journey in Latin America.[14] This trip offered him impressions, at a height of 1200 metres, on landscape and nature that he would implement in his urban-design theories over the following years.

14. Le Corbusier, *Précisions*, 3.

He specifies the idea of the bird's-eye view, or how "the airplane indicts" for his urban-design theories and projects as "[i]t is as an architect and town-planner-and therefore as a man essentially occupied with the welfare of his species-that I let myself be carried off on the wings of an airplane, make use of the bird's-eye view, of the view from the air, to which end I directed the pilot to steer over cities".[15]

In *La Ville Radieuse*, published in 1935, Le Corbusier recalls the words of Mermoz and de Saint-Exupéry, whom he met in the plane: "'Beware, Monsieur Le Corbusier, man has just acquired an eye situated at 4,000, 10,000 meters above the ground'. For years I have been using an eye that is ten thousand meters above the ground!"[16] But, from *using* the bird's-eye view for years, as he is saying – for example, by using aerial photography of the French air forces to draw his urban-design plans in 1925, which were exhibited at the L'Esprit Nouveau Pavilion – he now had the opportunity to *experience* it himself:

> [T]he bird's eye view. The eye now sees in substance what the mind formerly could only subjectively conceive. It is a new function added to our senses. It is a new standard of measurement. It is a new basis of sensation. Man will make use of it to conceive new aims. Cities will arise out of their ashes.[17]

Weissmann would have the occasion to experience for himself the bird's-eye view while sharing with Le Corbusier a short trip in an open aeroplane in Barcelona in March 1932, where they met again during the CIRPAC meeting organized by Josep Lluís Sert. He again captured the event, this time in photographs, as well as Barcelona and its surroundings seen from above, while Le Corbusier memorized it through his usual technique of sketching.

Le Corbusier (far left) taking a plane with Ernest Weissmann, to fly over Barcelona during the CIRPAC meeting in 1932

15. Le Corbusier, *Aircraft*, 5.

16. Le Corbusier and Philippe Duboÿ, *Aircraft* (Marseilles: Parenthèses, 2017), 112.

17. Le Corbusier, *Aircraft*, 96.

Brochure image of the second national congress on French aviation, 1946; Le Corbusier was, from the first congress in 1945, appointed president for the infrastructure section.

Sketch at the airport by Le Corbusier, 1946, published in the special issue of *L'Architecture d'aujourd'hui* on Le Corbusier in April 1948

Le Corbusier clearly acquired a taste for flying after his first experience, as the multiplication of his air trips in the following years testifies. Buenos Aires, Rio, Barcelona, Algiers, New York, and Chicago are only a few of the cities he saw from a plane in the following years. As his career and the geography of the projects expanded, the plane would become more and more a regular transport for him, to which another aspect would be added – that of a temporarily private "bubble". Once the project for Chandigarh started, he flew twice a year to India from 1951 until his death, for which he had almost always the same seat reserved with Air India. The first experience and the growing commodity to take a plane are also echoed in his architecture and urban-design projects and their representations, reflections on urban design, and participations and memberships in reflection groups on the urbanization of the air. Even though Le Corbusier was very critical about the geographical position of Le Bourget, he would in 1930 with Pierre Jeanneret design a pavilion for the Société des Transports Aériens Rapides (STAR) at Le Bourget and, when the competition for the new airport building was launched in 1935, Pierre Jeanneret and Le Corbusier initially aspired to participate – although they later resigned due to the unclear procedures of the contest.

This first great era of the full development of civil air traffic was still an era of risks. The planes often flew at very limited heights; they were subject to air turbulence; their insulation was lacking, resulting in a very low interior temperature; and there were huge noise levels and a strong smell of fuel. Although it was early June that day of his first flight, Le Corbusier left in a heavy coat to face the low temperatures in the plane. The risk of crashing was still very present at that time, as shown by the F-FARI plane he took: a few months later, the plane had several engine failures and crashed in October of that same year. It is not a coincidence that Le Corbusier, on the eve of his departure, sent an envelope containing his will to his brother Albert "to be opened in the event of Charles-Edouard Jeanneret's death".[18]

18. Letter from Le Corbusier to Albert Jeanneret, 5 June 1929 (FLC, R1-10-424 & 425).

Le Corbusier, smiling but nervous, just after he has handled the administration and visa for departure

Le Corbusier, seen from behind, taking the opportunity to check closely another Farman plane, the Jabiru

Le Corbusier, at right, and Pierre Jeanneret, at left, watching
a Farman Jabiru taking off for Brussels and Amsterdam

Pierre Jeanneret and Le Corbusier inspecting and wandering around the planes while waiting for his flight to Berlin

Le Corbusier and Pierre Jeanneret, at right, discussing with a pilot, at left; in the background, the famous hangars designed by Henry Lossier in 1921

Le Corbusier, in the middle of the image, and Pierre Jeanneret, at the extreme left, walk impatiently amongst the technical staff – one is pushing the staircase – to the Farman Goliath that will take Le Corbusier to Cologne and Berlin.

Weissmann films, with great attention, the technical details of the Goliath plane: the span of the wings, with motors and stressing cables.

Le Corbusier and Pierre Jeanneret, joking together with
Ernest Weissmann, as an "accomplice", behind the camera

Le Corbusier is boarding the plane; the small staircase needs to be held by the staff, and Le Corbusier must bend deeply to enter the plane through the small door.

The scale of the landing gears, held by wooden blocks,
and the vastness of the open surroundings – with,
at right, the Lossier hangars

After having filmed the details of the plane, Ernest Weissmann takes a step back to film the coherent technology of the plane.

The plane takes off from the mud at Le Bourget. Weissmann films Pierre Jeanneret waving at the plane as it flies away towards the horizon – not so different to waving off a departure by train.

3

The making of the Mundaneum diorama, Buttes-Chaumont, 20 & 21 July 1929

During a hot weekend in July, Le Corbusier, Pierre Jeanneret, and their collaborators realize a giant paintwork in a Gaumont film-set studio at Buttes-Chaumont in Paris: a large, coloured panorama on canvas of 10 by 5 metres presenting the urban-design project of the Cité Mondiale, which has to be shown in Geneva by the end of July 1929. The almost three minutes of film reels Ernest Weissmann shoots of the making of that diorama are an exceptional source, as the diorama itself, as well as the original photographs taken of the installation, have now been lost. Besides their documentary importance, the images also offer a unique opportunity to grasp the enthusiasm and commitment of the young architects and their masters working together on a project considered of major importance.

1:1000 plan of the Cité Mondiale, drawn in July 1928

The project of the Cité Mondiale was drawn up by Le Corbusier and Pierre Jeanneret in 1928, on the demand of Paul Otlet, who submitted a specific programme to the architects. Otlet had been pressed to host his 13.5 million documentation cards of the Palais Mondial, previously housed in the Palais du Cinquentenaire in Brussels, at a new site in Geneva. The urban-design plans were situated on the hillside of Grand-Saconnex-Prégny, north of the city of Geneva, and north towards the selected location for the new headquarters for the Society of Nations. The first contacts between Otlet and Le Corbusier date back to 1927, probably during the contest for the new Palace of the League of Nations, even if most probably they both were already aware of each other's work earlier on. By that time, Otlet had already devoted a big part of his life to the development of projects for a mondial city. A first collaboration with Hendrik Christian Andersen and Ernest Hébrard from 1910 until the outbreak of the First World War resulted in a totalitarian, Beaux-Arts-style urban-design project. After the First World War, Otlet took up his projects again, and shifted the attention from 1924 onwards from Brussels to the city of Geneva, with a new project for a mondial city that he presented there during a conference of the Union of International Associations (UAI), which he had founded in 1910. This shift seems logical, as the

Un record utile — pour une foi. !

Le patient horloger que l'on voit ici, amoureusement penché sur son travail, n'est autre que M. Charles Fleck, chef du service chronométrique de la fabrique de montres Zénith, au Locle. M. Fleck a établi récemment deux nouveaux records du monde pour la précision des chronomètres de bord et de poche aux observatoires de Teddington et de Neuchâtel. M. Fleck est parvenu, en effet, à limiter à 5 et 6 centièmes de seconde respectivement l'écart diurne moyen des chronomètres Zénith présentés à ces deux observatoires. (Photo H. Stauder, Zofingue)

La pose de la première pierre du Palais des Nations vue par les caricaturistes Derso et Kelen !

On reconnaît sans peine, parmi ces ouvriers comiquement affairés: 1. le khan Foroughi président du Conseil; 2. M. Guerrero, président de la Xme Assemblée; 3. M. Titulesco (Roumanie); 4. M. Stresemann; 5. sir E. Drummond, secrétaire général de la S. d. N.; 6. M. Scialoja (Italie); 7. M. Zaleski (Pologne); 8. M. Henderson (Gde-Bretagne); 9. M. MacDonald; 10. M. Adachi (Japon); 11. M. Briand; 12. lord R. Cecil (Gde-Bretagne); 13. M. Alb. Thomas, directeur du B. I. T.; 14. M. Hymans (Belgique); 15. M. Quinones de Léon (Espagne).

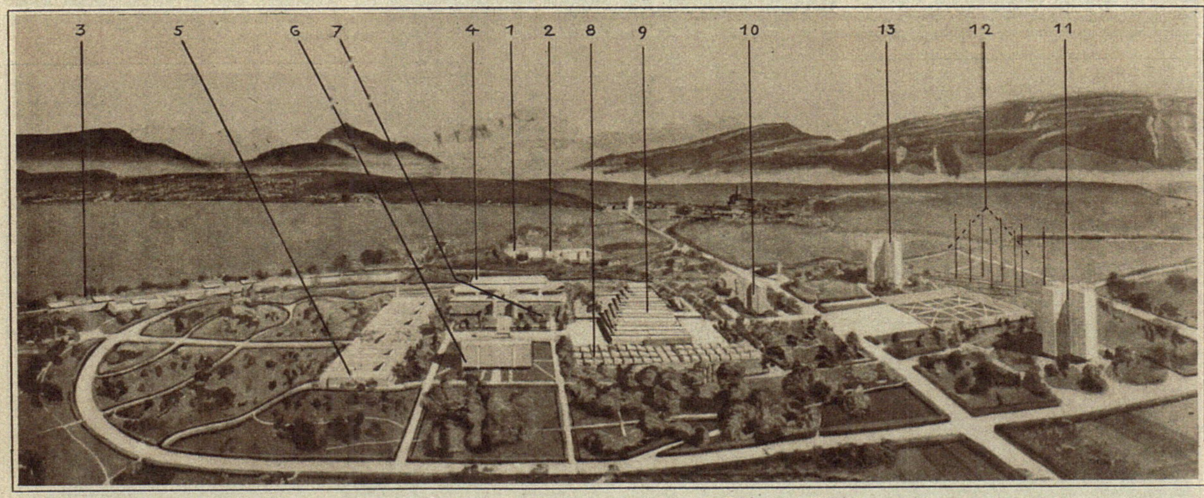

Le projet de Cité mondiale des architectes neuchâtelois Le Corbusier et P. Jeanneret.

Cette « cité mondiale » devrait s'élever près de Genève. Elle serait le centre universel où battrait le cœur de la civilisation nouvelle, qui se fonde sur la coopération des peuples. Là seraient réunis le B. I. T. (déjà existant), le Palais des Nations, la Banque internationale, la centrale des organisations de l'hygiène et le mundeanum, c'est-à-dire le quartier général du monde intellectuel. Telles sont, en quelques mots, les grandes lignes de cet intéressant projet qui est exposé actuellement à Genève. (1. Le B. I. T.; 2. la S. d. N.; 3. la Cité hôtelière; 4. le Stade; 5. le Palais des expositions des nations et des continents; 6. la Bibliothèque; 7. l'Université; 8. le Palais des expositions des Associations; 9. le Musée mondial; 10. la salle des congrès; 11. le bâtiment des trusts internationaux 12. le station de T. S. F., et 13. la Banque internationale.) (Photo Kettel, Genève)

A photograph of the diorama while displayed curved, used in the Swiss magazine ***L'Illustré*** and also taken up by Le Corbusier in the first volume of the ***Oeuvre complète***, is the only still-existing visual of the complete painted diorama.

League of Nations, on which Otlet worked intensively with Henri La Fontaine, had been founded in the aftermath of the First World War to ensure peace between nations; its headquarters had, since 1921, been situated in Geneva.

The Atelier Le Corbusier and Pierre Jeanneret realized two sets of plans for the project. After the realization of the first set of plans in summer 1928, Otlet published *Mundaneum*, on the Mondial City, in which the plans of Le Corbusier and Pierre Jeanneret were included. The plans were taken up again and further developed in February 1929, resulting in a second publication. The Atelier was thus working on the project with the hectic sequel of the competition for the Palace of the League of Nations in the background, and the importance Le Corbusier attributed to the displaying of the Mundaneum project with a large diorama is probably influenced by these events. All perspective drawings, and so also the diorama, focus on the importance of the wide view, from the hillside to the lake and the mountains behind. The pyramid-shaped Mundaneum building, in the centre of the Cité Mondiale, is described by Paul Otlet as “a symbol of intellectual unity of the World and Humanity”,[1] but its form will be much criticized by Le Corbusier's contemporaries, including his own collaborators.

Anticipating the 10th Assembly of the League of Nations at the end of summer 1929 in Geneva, which would include the laying of the foundation stone of the new headquarters in the Ariana Park, Paul Otlet insists on the importance of that event to claim their aspirations for the Mondial City. In addition to a petition and a congress of the UAI, Otlet plans from spring 1929 onwards an exhibition pavilion where a diorama, a model, and plans would show the urban-design project to

1. Boesiger, Willy and Oscar Stonorov, eds. *Le Corbusier et Pierre Jeanneret. Œuvre complète 1910-1929*. Third edition, 1943. (Zurich: Girsberger, 1930), 190.

Photograph of the diorama of 1922, depicting the Plan for a City of 3 Million Inhabitants

the congress members, the international members of the League of Nations, and the general public.[2] Le Corbusier had realized a first diorama of 1 by 1.5 metres on cardboard at the beginning of July,[3] but was convinced that, rather than a small or flat painting, a large, curved panorama on canvas as an immersive installation in itself was needed for maximal effect on the public. The idea of an immersive panoramic view to illustrate the urban-design plans of the Mondial City succeeded earlier dioramas Le Corbusier and Pierre Jeanneret had already created before. At the Paris Salon d'Automne of 1922 in the Grand Palais, Le Corbusier had presented for the first time a stand with a diorama illustrating his theoretical project, without a defined site, for his Plan for a City of 3 Million Inhabitants. Le Corbusier here took up the codes of 19th-century panorama installations representing magnificent city vistas and visuals of glorious events, but instead of showing an existing city view he created a city view of a possible future. This first diorama was about 16 m by 8 m, presented curved, offering the spectators in the middle of the stand an overwhelming view into this ideal city project. At both sides of the stand were presented some more plans and details of the project. The project thus doubled its effect on the visitor, firstly by presenting a city plan as urban project and not a model of urban decoration "such as a fountain, with the décor of a city in the background",[4] and secondly by taking up the 19th-century idea of a city panorama with a resolutely new content. The curved perspective system required on the flat canvas points out the difficulty in realizing a diorama: a curvilinear projective system needs to be used in order to perceive the curved canvas as a normal view, without distortion at the extremities of the drawing, once the canvas is installed in its curved position. Several documents and plans bear witness to the expertise of Le Corbusier and Pierre Jeanneret regarding the realization of the curvilinear perspective and the conception of the stand.[5] This diorama was carefully stored by Abel Gance in the Gaumont Studios, and taken up again in 1925 together with a new, complementary diorama of the Plan Voisin for Paris. If the structure of the first diorama of 1922 was still very rudimentary, both dioramas were now integrated into a real architectural project and presented face to face in the second space of the L'Esprit Nouveau Pavilion with the curved walls as devices for the dioramas.

Following these experiences, Le Corbusier would decide on a new stance with a diorama for the Cité Mondiale. Smaller than the two first dioramas of 1922 and 1925, the new diorama was imagined on a canvas of 10 m by 5 m. The preparation of the new diorama on the Cité Mondiale project was of major concern for the Atelier during the entire month of July, as Le Corbusier estimated the time of

2. Letter from Paul Otlet to Le Corbusier, 1 April 1929 (FLC, F-1-15-1).

3. Letter from Albert Jeanneret, on behalf of Le Corbusier, to Paul Otlet, 1 July 1929 (FLC, F1-14-2).

4. Le Corbusier, *Le Corbusier et Pierre Jeanneret. Œuvre complète 1910-1929*, 34.

5. Víctor Velásquez, "The Drawing of the Diorama of Le Corbusier and Pierre Jeanneret in 1922", *EGA. Revista de Expresión Gráfica Arquitectónica*, 2015.

The exhibition room of the L'Esprit Nouveau Pavilion in 1925 had curved walls used to hang the dioramas of the Plan Voisin and the Plan for a City of 3 Million Inhabitants.

realization to be about four days to address the technical outlines, to draw, and to paint. Besides the practical issues of finding the time for painting were added the requirements of the presentation of the diorama, the design, but, of course, also the construction of the pavilion housing it. A series of letters of Le Corbusier and Paul Otlet, written in preparation for the exhibition of the diorama, bears witness to how the project occupied them, and the correspondence of that period between Le Corbusier and his mother testifies to the intensity of preparation. In the week prior to the execution of the diorama canvas, Le Corbusier writes to Paul Otlet, "We are painting 1 diorama of $50m^2$ (10m long x 5m high). Must be arranged in a curve and seen from the stage. We will make 1 drawing of the set-up. Will send diorama + drawing to Edmond Wanner, friend and client. Expect to finish and send this Saturday."[6]

The importance of the arc for the panoramic perception of the painting is illustrated with a small sketch of the curved wall that was needed to display the diorama. Le Corbusier would insist on the right viewing perspective later while the diorama was exposed at Geneva, when he asked Otlet for a photograph of the curved diorama in which the deformation of the view when the canvas was flat would not be noticeable. As only preparatory drawings of the panoramic view still exist, the curved perspective view of the Mondial City, where the encircling roads are very curved instead of horizontal, has become today the standard view. The pavilion installation

Perspective drawing of the Cité Mondiale realized in 1929, which served as a basis for the diorama painting

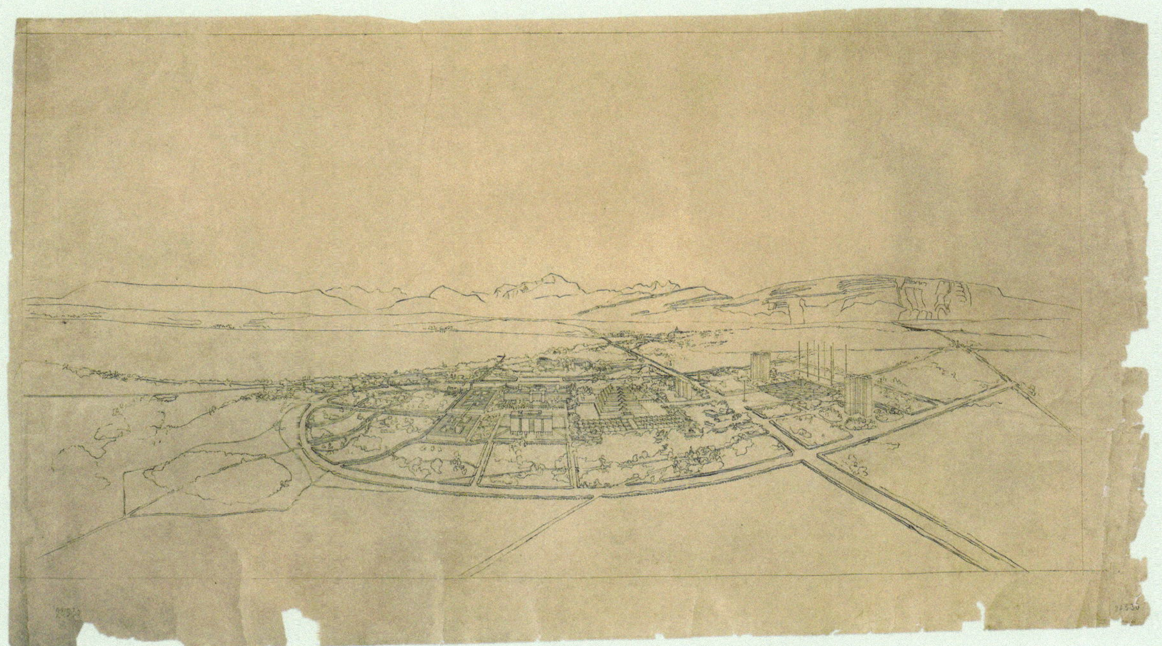

6. Letter from Le Corbusier to Paul Otlet, 18 July 1929 (FLC, F1-15-130).

therefore required specific adaptations to correctly hang the canvas in an arc, with a stage and a bench for contemplation by visitors. The pavilion was planned by Le Corbusier as a prefabricated construction to be executed by Edmond Wanner, client and builder of the then-ongoing Maison Clarté project at Geneva.

Le Corbusier, Pierre Jeanneret, and at least five other persons – out of whom we can recognize their collaborators Charlotte Perriand and Kunio Maekawa – spent the weekend of 20 to 22 July together to finally paint the diorama of the Mondial City. Le Corbusier described the collective enthusiasm of these three exceptional days to his mother and brother, as well as his conclusion about the lost competition on the new Palace of the League of Nations building:

> We had to do a giant job: a 10.45m diorama representing the Cité Mondiale and the whole canton of Geneva, Mt Blanc etc. This was done in very hot conditions in a hangar in the Buttes-Chaumont where the temperature was frightening. Never have I been so overwhelmed, so exhausted, as during these three days, because it was necessary to work double-time, so vast and meticulous was the work. Finally, the diorama left on Monday. St Paul's will make a home for it in Geneva, and tongues can start wagging. This is the clear visualisation of all the plans made over the last two years. There, everyone can read, reconstruct, understand. And as it is large, "natural" and in colour, it seduces. A large congress of fifteen hundred international people will be marching in front of it. Then, in September, it will be the delegates of the League of Nations. The Palace is finished for us.[7]

Weissmann films the extraordinary work of the diorama at several moments during the weekend. He marks the beginning of the work, filming the drawing that is to be enlarged, and concludes at the end of the weekend with the result by taking from height a slow, panoramic shot of the enlarged copy. Between the two views of the small painting at the beginning and the large painting at the end, he films moments of work, of supreme concentration, and overall fatigue. His sequences also illustrate the practice of the enlargement of the painting: the dividing of the canvas into small squares, after which the content of the small painting could be meticulously copied and painted onto the immense canvas. The tasks of enlargement, drawing, and painting are sometimes seen simultaneously: sequences show how Pierre Jeanneret is drawing in the squares while Le Corbusier is already painting the mountains. The filmed shots of Le Corbusier, Pierre Jeanneret, and the collaborators – for example Charlotte Perriand, recognizable by her necklace – with drawing tools and brushes give us an insight into the process of making the diorama, and show an arduous work carried out in an atmosphere of supreme concentration, conviviality, and enthusiasm. The location and working conditions can be perceived by the general views, showing the interior of the hangar; several elements that seem to be cinema sets; the tripod with the small diorama to be enlarged; the enlargement tools; the paint pots and big brushes; and, above all, a large floor available to lay out the canvas on which the diorama is being painted.

7. Letter from Le Corbusier and Yvonne to his mother and Albert, 26 July 1929 (Le Corbusier, Rémi Baudouï, and Arnaud Dercelles, *Correspondance. Lettres à la famille. Tome I: 1900-1925* [Gollion: Infolio, 2011], 220).

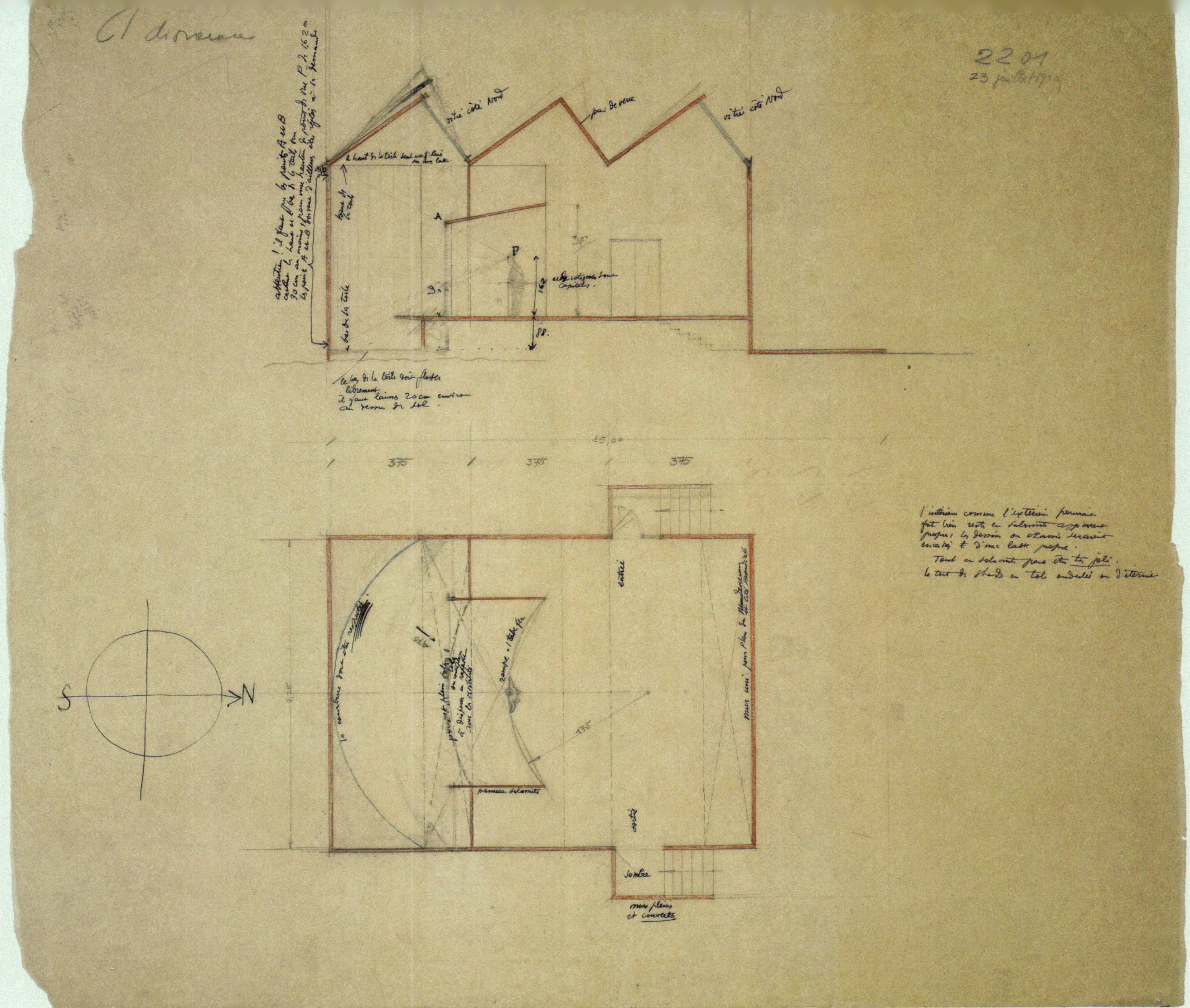

Plans for the pavilion for the Cité Mondiale diorama – drawn by Ernest Weissmann the day after the weekend of painting, and sent immediately to Geneva

The diorama was – of course – not ready on the Saturday as promised by Le Corbusier. He added to his letter to Otlet, “We are exhausted! The temperature in our hangar at [Avenue] Bolivar is terrible!”[8]

This fatigue, from the non-stop work and the heat, is clearly perceptible in Weissmann's images. The first images show the masters and collaborators in full energy and well dressed. As the weekend progresses, fatigue and heat become more and more visible in the images: shirts are drowned by sweat or taken off, sweat on the faces, arms outstretched and even Charlotte Perriand lying on the diorama for a little nap. Immediately after the weekend, on Monday and Tuesday, Weissmann drew the design of the pavilion in which the diorama with the plans of the Cité Mondiale would be displayed. No break was allowed after the exhausting weekend. The plan of the pavilion, the diorama and the plans to be exhibited were sent to Edmond Wanner in Geneva the day Weissmann finished the plans. Le Corbusier and his wife, Yvonne, and Pierre Jeanneret left the next day for Piquey, where they spent their holidays until 20 August. The rest of the event was then in the hands of Paul Otlet: to look for the exact location, make contacts with the contractors to have the small pavilion built, prepare and expose all material sent

8. Letter from Le Corbusier to Paul Otlet, 18 July 1929 (FLC, F1-15-130).

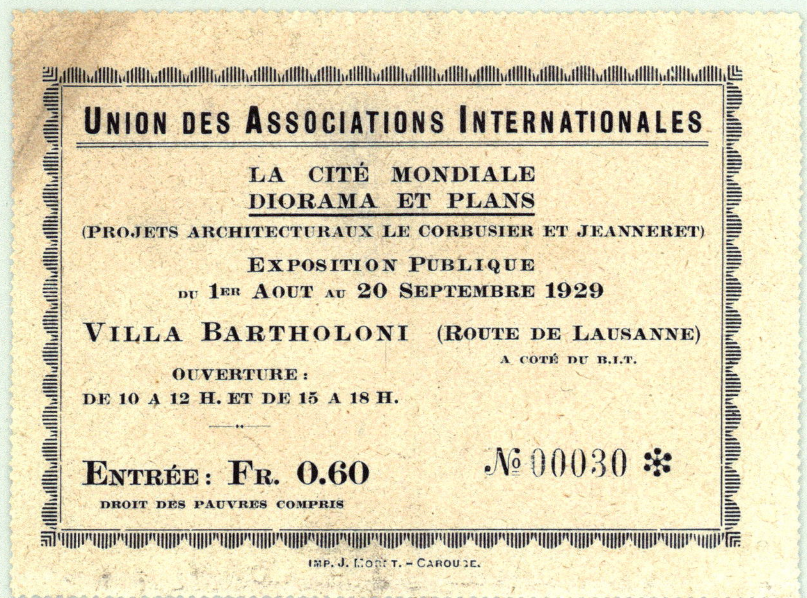
UNION DES ASSOCIATIONS INTERNATIONALES

LA CITÉ MONDIALE
DIORAMA ET PLANS
(PROJETS ARCHITECTURAUX LE CORBUSIER ET JEANNERET)

EXPOSITION PUBLIQUE
DU 1ER AOUT AU 20 SEPTEMBRE 1929

VILLA BARTHOLONI (ROUTE DE LAUSANNE)
A COTÉ DU B.I.T.

OUVERTURE :
DE 10 A 12 H. ET DE 15 A 18 H.

ENTRÉE : FR. 0.60
DROIT DES PAUVRES COMPRIS

№ 00030

Entrance ticket for the pavilion, a "public exhibition" of the diorama and the plans of the Cité Mondiale

by Le Corbusier, host the congress of the UAI, and undertake all the necessary publicity. The final location was no longer a garden in front of the Carlton Hotel – and therefore opposite the Ariana Park, where the Palace of the League of Nations was to be built – but the garden of the Villa Bartholoni, where Paul Otlet was also preparing the meetings and lectures for the UAI Congress. Even though there is no doubt that a pavilion was built, it is until today not certain which contractor was assigned and whether it was built following the plans of the Atelier.[9] But the pavilion was, not surprisingly, not finished for the congress, which was only a week after sending the documents. The UAI members could, during their congress, admire only the small painting that was presented in the villa.

The 10th Assembly of the League of Nations at the beginning of September was for Paul Otlet and Le Corbusier, who would travel to Geneva for the occasion, the opportunity to show the delegates the diorama and the plans of the Cité Mondiale. Le Corbusier met several personalities, amongst them the French politicians Louis Loucheur and Aristide Briand, who delivered during that assembly his famous speech wherein he proposed a federal union of European nations. The importance for Le Corbusier of discussing with the delegates of the League of Nations his urban plans, and probably his ideas in a more general way, is reflected in the caption he wrote for the full-page diorama photograph on the last page of the first volume of the *Œuvre complète* of Le Corbusier and Pierre Jeanneret.[10] Le Corbusier was finalizing the first volume at the same time as they were working on the creation and presentation of the diorama in Geneva, and probably inserted the photograph at the very end of the book project as the chapter on the Mundaneum project, covering eight pages, is displayed earlier in the book, before such projects as the Villa Church in Ville d'Avray and the Centrosoyus. It is the same image that was used by the magazine *L'Illustré* pointing out for its readers the different components of the city. This photograph of the exhibited canvas, made by the Swiss photographer Max Kettel, is the only tangible record of the hard work that went into the preparations for this ephemeral event. Barely a week after Le Corbusier returned from Geneva, he took the SS *Massilia* ocean liner to Brazil on 14 September. On the agenda were a series of conferences on architecture and urbanism in Buenos Aires, Rio de Janeiro, São Paulo, and Montevideo in the space of two months, which he would afterwards publish in his book *Précisions*.[11] During the transatlantic voyage, he wrote several letters wherein he impresses on his addressees the importance of the diorama. The current events surrounding the League of Nations, the assembly and decisions on the new headquarters location, also led him to dedicate the first part of one of his last

9. A blueprint in the archives of Paul Otlet presents the stamp of the Solomite company accompanied by the signature of the architect, F. Quétant (Mundaneum Mons, PP PO D8 002).

10. Le Corbusier, *Le Corbusier et Pierre Jeanneret. Œuvre complète 1910-1929*, 214.

11. Le Corbusier, *Précisions sur un état présent de l'architecture et de l'urbanisme* (Paris: Les Éditions G. Crès & Cie, 1930).

Hélène de Mandrot, Le Corbusier, and Paul Otlet, sitting on a bench overlooking Lake Geneva after visiting the diorama and explaining the project to Mme de Mandrot

lectures, given at the Faculty of Sciences in Buenos Aires on Thursday, 17 October 1929, to the topic: "La 'Cité Mondiale' et considérations peut-être inopportunes".[12]

The legend that is told is that Paul Otlet brought the diorama back to Belgium and stored it in the Pavilion of Human Passions in Brussels, a work by Victor Horta and Jef Lambeaux close to the Palais du Cinquentenaire, which hosted the Palais Mondial of Otlet until 1934, but that it has since disappeared. More probable is that Otlet stored the diorama in his Palais Mondial and that it was lost after the expulsion of his Palais Mondial from the Palais du Cinquentenaire. The fate of the diorama was thus no different from that of the previous dioramas of 1922 and 1925 by the Atelier Le Corbusier and Pierre Jeanneret, which were also lost. Only the diorama of the Macià Plan presented in 1934 at the *La Nova Barcelona* exhibition survives. Although it is much smaller in scale, and not painted by Le Corbusier and Pierre Jeanneret,[13] it can still give us a glimpse of ten years of perspective-painting practice. One could question if the other dioramas were lost despite or because of their large size. There are few documents today that tell us the story of the creation and presentation of the Cité Mondiale diorama. However, by pooling information from the four projects, it is possible to sketch out a working method and an acquired experience – both for the dioramas and for their exhibition constructions. The views taken by Weissmann during the realization of the Cité Mondiale diorama are thus important in the narrative of the Cité Mondiale project and in the larger chain of the creation of the drawing and hanging structures of the dioramas, as they contain valuable information about the project. However, they also transgress their subject matter and tell us other stories: of dedicated architects and collaborators, and of a painstaking presentation practice that we can no longer imagine today.

12. "Le Corbusier, *Précisions*, 215–32.

13. This diorama was only 6 by 1.5 m, and fitted in a circular screen of 5 m diameter (José Ramon Alonso Pereira, "Le Corbusier's dioramas", *Cuadernos de Proyectos Arquitectonicos*, no. 4, 2013, 135).

Pierre Jeanneret tracing squares on the canvas to enlarge the Cité Mondiale painting, showing the laborious preparation before painting

Ernest Weissmann captures in one image the size of the small painting and the canvas on the ground measuring 5 by 10 m, with five persons sitting and working on it.

Charlotte Perriand and Kunio Maekawa on the right, and another collaborator on the left, working on the canvas

A filmed viewpoint from ground level, with everyone working in deepest concentration; Le Corbusier in the foreground, stood painting

Pierre Jeanneret, Kunio Maekawa, and another collaborator tracing and drawing on the canvas; the mountains, the large slice in the middle of the canvas, have already been painted.

Le Corbusier painting, with large sweeps, on the canvas

Le Corbusier standing on the almost-finished canvas with a pot of paint in his hands, reviewing the work

Charlotte Perriand lying on the finished painting, exhausted by the work of the weekend, with Le Corbusier passing by

Pierre Jeanneret, exhausted, without shirt because of the heat, checking the enlargement; Le Corbusier clearing up paint pots

Charlotte Perriand, always recognizable by her necklace, walking on the painting

The diorama almost finished: Charlotte Perriand still doing some fine-tuning seated in the middle on the canvas; the others, Pierre Jeanneret and Le Corbusier at left, and Kunio Maekawa at right, reviewing the results of the weekend

4

Enjoying Paris, 1929-1930

Staying in Paris during his internship at Le Corbusier's and Pierre Jeanneret's office also gives Weissmann, and his friends, the opportunity to visit and experience the architecture projects of their masters and to enjoy numerous events in the city. Although Weissmann has already been in Paris from the end of 1926, where he first worked at Adolf Loos's office, acquiring the film camera in 1929 is an occasion to look with fresh eyes at the city and capture events as well as some daily situations of life in the city, which often function as a visual confirmation of his ideas and preoccupations and those of his masters.

The reels with special moments from the Atelier captured by Weissmann are interspersed with sequences depicting situations from everyday life and events he and his friends enjoyed, such as street impressions, workmen on construction sites, the automobile and boat exhibitions in the Grand Palais, the aviation meeting in Vincennes, or football games. They give an informal insight into how immense and immersive the experience was of working at the Atelier Le Corbusier and Pierre Jeanneret. Visiting the projects of his masters provided some special moments he captured on film, although in rather condensed sequences. Among these visits, Nikolai Kolli's stay in Paris in winter 1929–30 offers some exceptional images. Kolli, a Russian architect who spoke French, was sent in December 1928 by the Centrosoyus to the Atelier Le Corbusier and Pierre Jeanneret for the further elaboration of the construction plans of their building, and became a key figure in the following-up of the construction in Moscow. The contract between the Centrosoyus and the architects stipulated particularly that they had to initiate him in the modern architecture of France. Le Corbusier and Pierre Jeanneret did so by visiting works by Gustave Lyon with him soon after his first arrival.[1] Weissmann accompanied Kolli to several events in Paris, which were larger in scope than the recent architecture productions. Some film sequences, for example, show Kolli present in the Colombes tribune watching the football match for the Coup de France 1929/1930 featuring the very popular Racing Club de France, where Weissmann tried to take a "selfie" with his camera turned on both of them. Together, they visited the Asile Flottant barge *Louise Cathérine* of the Salvation Army in the presence of Albin Peyron, the commander of the French Salvation Army, two other officers, and Pierre Jeanneret. This 80 m long former cement barge had been bought in 1929 by Albin Peyron to be transformed by the architects into a floating refuge for 160 homeless people, providing beds, toilets, and kitchen facilities during winter months. Le Corbusier and Pierre Jeanneret had previously realized, in 1926, the Palais du Peuple for the Salvation Army, and discussions had already started with them for the Cité de Refuge. The transformation of the boat was an unusual architectural project as it cannot be considered a *building* in general terms, although the modifications to the barge were very structural and reflected their ideas on modern architecture by opening up the space, adding columns, large window bays, and a roof terrace. The works took place in autumn 1929, and, as Le Corbusier was on his tour of South America, Pierre Jeanneret often inspected the site works alone or with Albin Peyron. Shortly before the barge's inauguration on New Year's Day 1930, Weissmann captures their visit to the barge, moored on the Seine under the

1. Jean-Louis Cohen, *Le Corbusier et la mystique de l'U.R.S.S.* (Brussels: Mardaga, 1987), 108.

Perspective of the transformation of the barge into the Asile Flottant, 1929

Dormitory inside the Asile Flottant barge, revealing the new, well-lit spaces created by the architects

Front façade of the Villa Stein-de Monzie, photographed in 1928, Michael Stein's car prominently present linking the modernity of the car with the house

Pont d'Austerlitz. Workers are occupied painting the outside of the barge. Kolli is filmed as a very important figure, more so than Peyron, and this illustrates how much the Russian architect was appreciated by the Atelier.

In contrast to the off-the-record insight Weissmann offers of the building-site visit to the barge, the reels of a visit to the Villa Stein-de Monzie in mid-1929 express a focus on the architecture itself. Here, Weissmann concentrates his film sequences on the façade and the roof-terrace experience. He assimilates the human eye with his camera, and films as he is wandering on the roof terrace. However, he experiences difficulty in assimilating the narrow-angle view of the camera with the large viewing experience of the roof terrace. Josep Lluís Sert and Eugene Rosenberg, also present during the visit, are almost accidently filmed owing to the movement of his eye and, thus, also the camera. Weissmann further experiences the approach up the spiral stairs to the observation point, always on the move, looking how the camera could record the "scenery" of the architecture. By this way of filming, Weissmann experiments literally with Le Corbusier's much-remarked-upon idea of movement:

> Everything, including architecture, is a question of circulation. Let us not forget that, always present before us, a man must be standing on his legs, with his eyes at 1m70, looking, seeing, perceiving, transmitting to the intellectual and emotive mechanism images that have entered through this admirable machine of the eye.[2]

The Villa Stein-de Monzie was a sought-after project to visit from its completion in 1928 onwards. Extensive coverage in the architecture press, such as that by Sigfried Giedion and Christian Zervos in *Cahiers d'art* in 1928 and by Jean Badovici in *L'Architecture vivante* in 1928, as well as being one of the three villas presented in the film *Architecture d'aujourd'hui* by Pierre Chenal in 1931, enhanced its reputation. This visit by Weissmann was, however, not his first to the Villa, as he had already

2. Le Corbusier, *Une maison - un palais. À la recherche d'une unité architecturale*, Collection de "L'Esprit Nouveau" (Paris: Les Éditions G. Crès & Cie, 1928), 78.

been there a year before on 1 July 1928 in the company of Alfred Roth, Mart Stam, and Piet Mondrian. The family Stein and de Monzie opened their house regularly to colleagues and friends of Le Corbusier and Pierre Jeanneret, for example Alvar and Aino Aalto, who visited the Villa in the summer of 1928 during their journey to France, and, in September of that year, Mart Stam and Piet Mondrian returned to the Villa accompanied by the masters Sigfried Giedion; Georges Vantongerloo; and El Lissitzky and his wife, Sophie Lissitzky-Küppers. All photographed their presence at the Villa, capturing the allure of this monument for the modern times. The Steins were indeed very proud of their Villa, and the son Julian Stein would, the same summer of 1928, film with a 16 mm camera a visit by his aunt Gertrude Stein to the house. But they all captured only the exterior of the Villa, its façades, and especially its roof terraces, probably shocked by the contrast between the avant-garde house and the old-fashioned furniture inside.

Visit of Piet Mondrian (at the bottom of the stairs), Mart Stam, Georges Vantongerloo, Sophie Lissitzky-Küppers and El Lissitzky; Sophie Stein stands in the door opening

Joyfulness at visiting the works of their masters completes recorded daily scenes, of which one can sometimes only guess why Weissmann took an interest in filming them. Several sequences are dedicated to construction sites, filmed when exploring Paris. His focus on the act of constructing goes beyond the fact of the building and often expresses the human conditions of this hard labour: how four workmen lift a huge chunk of stone, how they rebuild a street, etc. But he also focuses on the techniques of building, the machines used for rebuilding the street, or the possibilities that the large reach of a crane offers on the building site. This interest is reflected in the sequences on the Villa Savoye, but also in the photographs – rather than film sequences – Weissmann took two years later of the building site of the Cité de Refuge. Some sequences filmed in Paris come close to the framing of a photograph, for example wandering through the city and capturing the light through the trees on an empty street. The poetic silence of these filmed photographs contrasts with the sequence he filmed of the chaotic street scenes in Paris from the Rolls-Royce of Sert on their way to the Villa Savoye in May 1929. Heading from the Pont de la Concorde to the Place de la Concorde,

Interior view of the 23rd Salon de l'Automobile in the Grand Palais in October 1929

Weissmann films the terrible situation of blocked circulation in the centre of the city. It recalls the ideas of Le Corbusier on the congestion of Paris, as in his 1925 publication *Urbanisme*, where newspaper clippings illustrate the traffic problems of Paris and he argues,

> Wherever one looks, there is congestion and suffocation. Where do the thousands of cars of the modern city stop? Along the pavements, jamming up traffic; traffic kills traffic: the New York businessman abandons his car in the suburbs![3]

Le Corbusier proves his assertions with two postcards of the Place de la Concorde illustrating the rapid increase of cars in the city, as 15 years earlier barely any car is present on the place. From his publications *Urbanisme* to *La Ville Radieuse* ten years later, Le Corbusier drew on the importance of the subject. The generously dimensioned circulation systems as drawn in the Plan Voisin and the City of 3 Million Inhabitants were his answer to the problem. The chaotic circulation captured by Weissmann, with even a policeman and a pedestrian standing and discussing amongst all the cars, cannot better demonstrate the need to perceive

3. Le Corbusier, *Urbanisme*, Collection de "L'Esprit Nouveau" (Paris: Les Éditions G. Crès & Cie, 1925), 110.

the street as a "machine to circulate".[4] Weissmann also shared with Le Corbusier and Pierre Jeanneret his fascination for new techniques, and so for cars. Not a Rolls, considered a luxurious but old-fashioned automobile, but the esthetical and technically advanced Voisin was the car preferred by his masters. It is in fact their vehicle one can often distinguish in published photographs of the villas, illustrating the analogy between the new techniques of the car and the new way of building. Their mutual attraction for cars drew Weissmann to abundantly film the Salon de l'Automobile in the Grand Palais that took place in October 1929. His attention is not so much on the Art Deco interior decorations of André Granet but on the overwhelming quantity of cars and visitors, and the thrilling technical innovations on display. As the panoramic views of the large hall of the Grand Palais more closely reflect his own impressions, he fully explores the capacity of his camera by filming the exposed engines in action. Fascinated by the new technologies of transport, he also visited the aviation meeting in Vincennes, and even the Salon Nautique earlier that year. Working at the Atelier was much more than producing architecture; it was an immersive "bath" of ideas on the possibilities of a thrilling future, brought to life by the events he enjoyed with his masters and friends in Paris.

Postcard from 1909 of the Place de la Concorde, used in 1925 by Le Corbusier to illustrate his statistics on the congestion of Paris in *Urbanisme*

4. Le Corbusier, *Urbanisme*, 110.

Summer view in a quiet Parisian street; the low sun slants between the buildings across the street.

Winter view in front of the café Les Deux Magots, the favourite bar of Le Corbusier and Pierre Jeanneret, and the Boulevard Saint-Germain at the left

Heading from the Pont de la Concorde to he Place de la Concorde, stuck in traffic, filmed from the Rolls-Royce of Josep Lluís Sert

The chaotic traffic at the Place de la Concorde, with two policemen trying to regulate proceedings

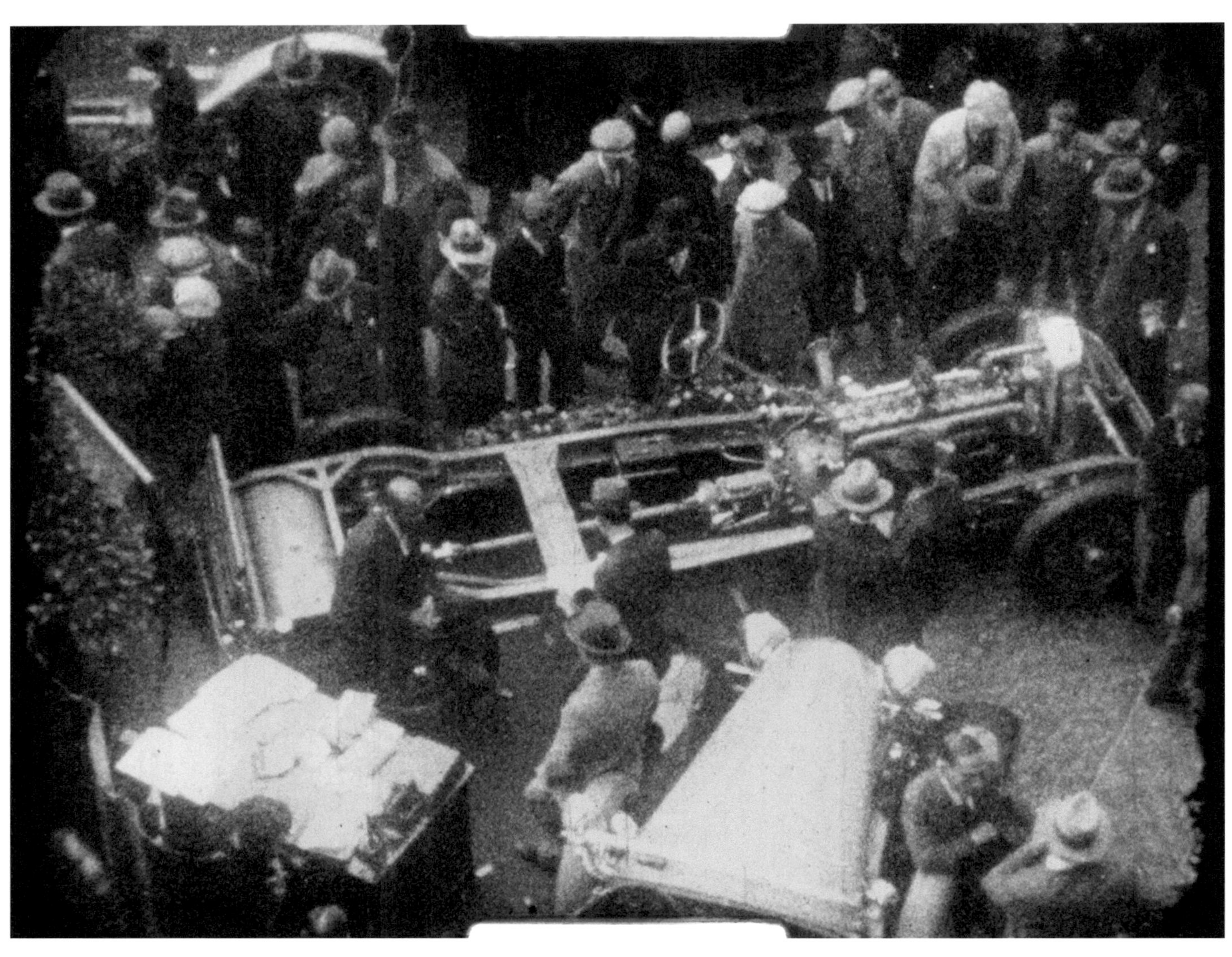

People gathering around the frame and engine of a dismantled car at the 23rd Salon de l'Automobile, Grand Palais

Close-up of a car engine at the 23rd Salon de l Automobile
in the Grand Palais

The upper balcony of the front façade of the Villa Stein-de Monzie, an unusual view where one can fully appreciate the spatial construction as a geometrical shell

Starting sequence of the stairs of the Villa Stein-de Monzie, leading to the house's highest observation terrace

Tall crane on the construction site of a 7-storey concrete building

Workmen during street works; the middle one puts his tongue out to the camera.

Nikolai Kolli and Ernest Weissmann on the deck of the Asile Flottant; Weissmann is holding a rolled journal paper, probably with plans.

Pierre Jeanneret (second from left) discussing the works of the Asile Flottant with Albin Peyron (second from right) and two other officers of the Salvation Army under the Pont d'Austerlitz; a homeless person (at the extreme left) observes the group

Nikolai Kolli on the deck of the Asile Flottant

Other barges moored next to the Asile Flottant on the Seine.

Visiting the building site of the Villa Savoye, 1929–1930

The year 1929 marks the launch of the construction of the Villa Savoye, which will become one of the most emblematic of Le Corbusier's and Pierre Jeanneret's projects and will also mark the end of a decade of intensive conceptualizations of modern individual houses. The building site offers collaborators, friends, and colleagues an opportunity to grasp the evolution from paper to building. Ernest Weissmann covers the construction site from the structural works in May 1929 until the finishing works at the end of May 1930, just before he leaves Paris for Zagreb. During one year, at least five site visits are captured on film in the company of his masters, his friends, and Sigfried Giedion. Even if Weissmann never edits this film footage together as a thematic event, by keeping the loose film reels – capturing moments of interest – his willingness to document the construction over time witnesses the fascination the project holds for everyone involved.

If today the Villa Savoye is seen as one of the most iconic houses of modernism, nothing hinted at this when Mme Savoye contacted Le Corbusier and Pierre Jeanneret in the late summer of 1928 with her request to build a "maison de campagne". The first plans the architects submitted to the client in October 1928 already showed the elevated box with a window strip all around and a curved upper storey, in the middle of the site. In March 1929, the construction could start after the approval for the works of the contractor, Cormier, known by M. Savoye. The construction progressed at great pace, as only two months later foundations and columns on the ground floor were finished and the scaffolding was prepared up to the first floor. During the spring and summer of 1929, Weissmann filmed at least three moments in the evolution of the structural work of the Villa Savoye, in the company of his friends and his masters. In January and May 1930, when the construction neared its end, he filmed the finishing works during two site visits (not with his masters this time but with their friend, the Swiss art critic Sigfried Giedion). Through time and through the different reels we glimpse the fascination and excitement for the construction of the Villa, on the part of Weissmann but also of Giedion and the other collaborators, against the background of numerous problems due to the surprisingly traditional execution methods, and the modifications and complications that had to be resolved during the construction.

When Weissmann decided in May 1929 to film the building site for the first time, the visit was made without Pierre Jeanneret or Le Corbusier, who was abroad at that moment. Instead, the visit was undertaken with his close group of collaborators: Josep Lluís Sert, Norman Rice, and Kunio Maekawa. Albert Frey did not seem to take part, even if he drew many of the plans of the house. The absence of the masters probably explains why a series of photographs of progress at the building site and of details has been taken, as it could have been a supplementary reason for Weissmann to document on film the construction. Weissmann also highlights all the technical aspects of the building process and constantly shows the workmen in action, especially during the erection of the structure in 1929. Several shots show construction details we are not used to seeing in photographs

Opposite page: Drawing by Le Corbusier of the key ideas behind the Villa Savoye, published in *Précisions* in 1930 after being drawn for a conference in Buenos Aires

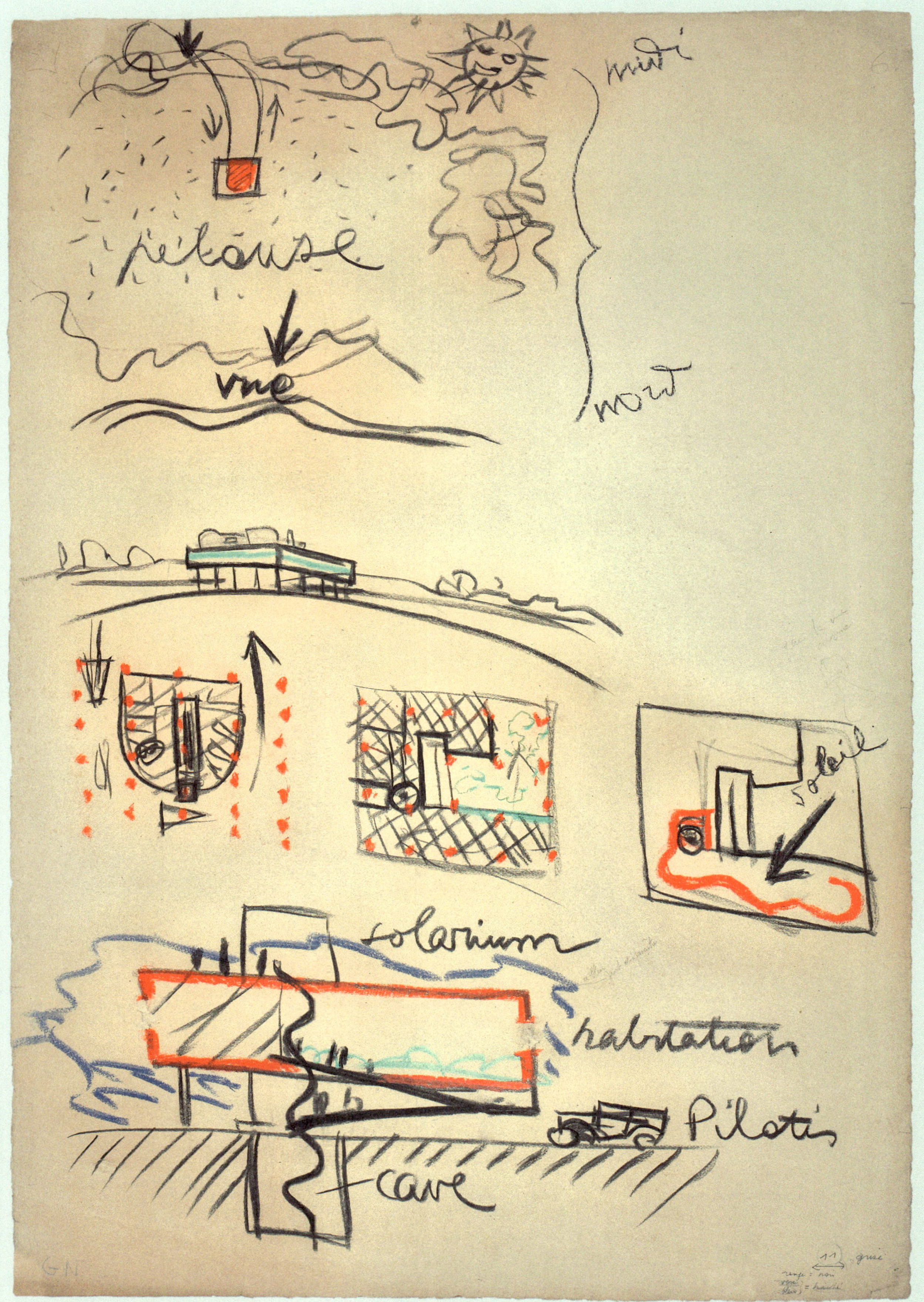
midi
pelouse
vue
nord
soleil
solarium
habitation
Pilotis
cave

or in professional documentary films of that period. Weissmann takes the time to film how the workmen cut and fold the steel reinforcement bars on site and how they place them. He witnesses the hard labour of preparing the concrete, bringing it up to the first floor by barrow and a manual pulley, the dumping – concrete then wasn't as liquid as it is today – in the concrete shuttering, and the manual vibrating to densify the concrete. He also films the fabrication of cement bricks, the masonry and types of hollow bricks, the timber formwork of the concrete *pilotis*, etc. Such a focus is certainly due to Weissmann's experience at the technical school in Zagreb and interest in construction detailing. His personal interest in the execution of architecture also appears through his human approach to the workers. Besides their technical work, he also portrays their faces – laughing – personalizing them as equals, which certainly reflects his communist preoccupations.

The footage also shows moments of pleasure with the other collaborators on site. Weissmann films their exploration of the building site, with Sert at the bottom of the ladder or Sert, Maekawa, and Rice taking pictures of the building site. One can imagine how after this scene Rice hurries down the building site to photograph a general view of the façade under construction, with the three others posing for the camera. In the picture of the three collaborators on the scaffolding that Rice takes, we can clearly identify Weissmann holding his camera; the film reels actually show Rice taking that photograph. The reels also capture in another way the pleasure and uniqueness the collaborators experienced together during their more than one hour excursion to Poissy, in the suburbs of Paris, as not only is the building site abundantly filmed but so too is the trip itself. Filmed inside Sert's car, his parents' Silver Ghost Rolls-Royce, the footage witnesses the liberty it offered them of escaping the dense traffic at the Place de la Concorde, heading to the green suburbs, and speeding along the road. The privileged viewpoint is from the seat next to the driver, with the *Flying Lady* figurine on the bonnet in frame, but also from the side windows, which better documents the speed of the car. Weissmann would repeat the filming of the trip to Poissy in January 1930 – but this time it is the Voisin mascot, of the car of Le Corbusier and Pierre Jeanneret, that is in frame.

Kunio Maekawa, Josep Lluís Sert, and Ernest Weissmann are pictured on the scaffolding of the Villa Savoye. Weissmann is holding his camera and filming Norman Rice, who is taking the photograph.

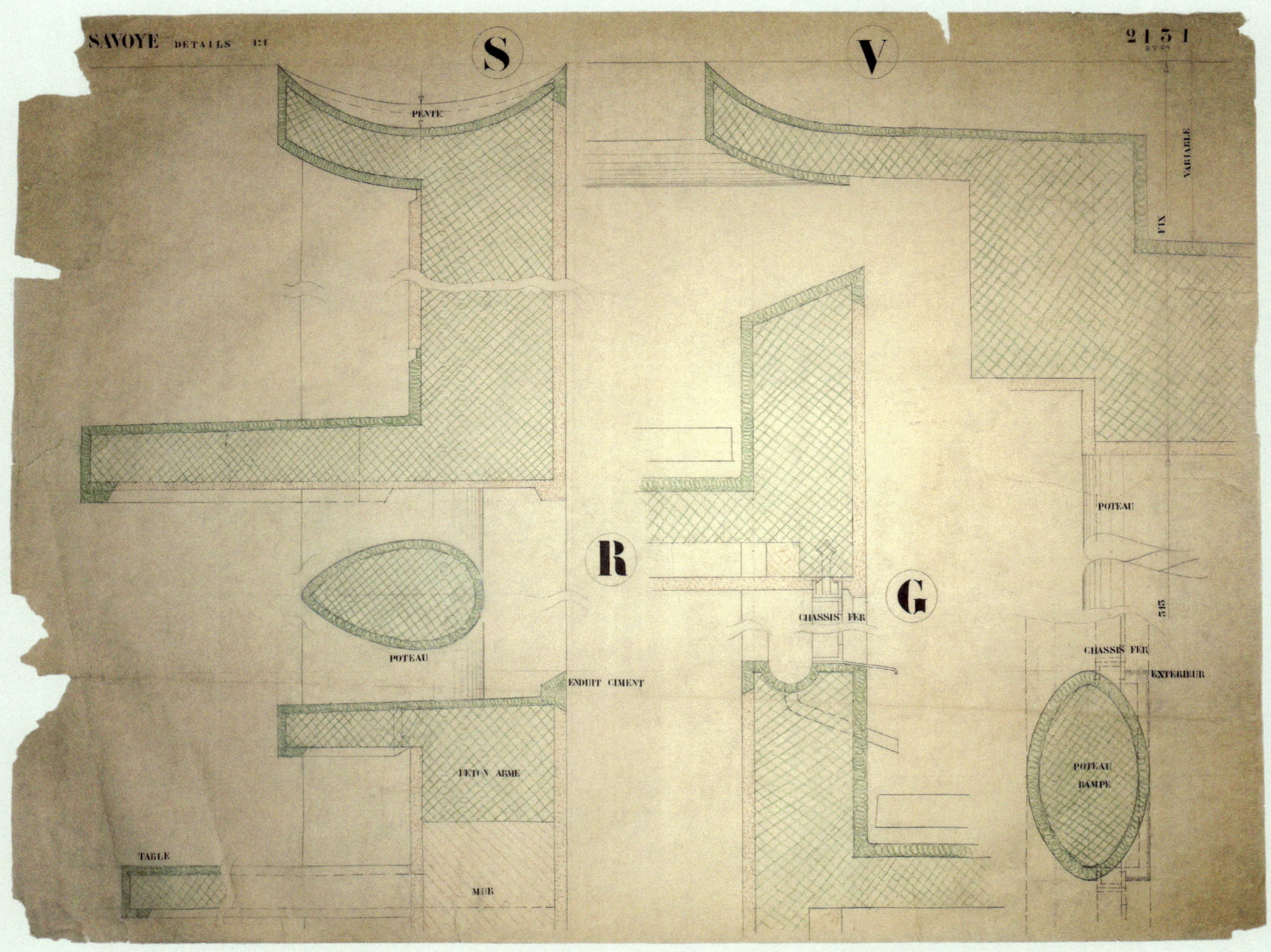

Details of the particular forms of the concrete ledges, beams, and columns, drawn by Albert Frey in May 1929; the discussion of these details between the architects and the contractor is filmed by Ernest Weissmann.

On the next two site visits he filmed – on 23 July, just after having finished the diorama canvas of the Cité Mondiale and the drawings of its shed, and on 24 August 1929 – Weissmann offers scenes that go beyond the pure recording of the architectural object, giving a unique insight into the supervision of the building site by the Atelier Le Corbusier and Pierre Jeanneret. He closely follows his masters with his camera inside the building under construction for the general inspection of the works, and captures their discussions in the heat of the moment as problems and modifications from the three parties – the Atelier, the contractor, and the client – are not uncommon during these months: delays with the subcontractors; errors in the placement of the frames; modifications requested by Mme Savoye; plan modifications by the Atelier, such as turning the service stairs; dimensional errors, which lead to problems with the frames; concerns from M. Savoye about the thinness of the partition walls; etc. The architects remain optimistic: "this morning we went to Poissy, the house is looking very good",[1] Jeanneret writes after their visit of 23 July to reassure M. Savoye. Weissmann films their gestures and dialogues while they discuss details, plans, and execution modes with the general contractor, Cormier; "after returning from holidays we went to Poissy where we discussed the various issues of concern to you",[2] Jeanneret updated the client on the situation.

1. Letter from Pierre Jeanneret to M. Savoye, 22 July 1929 (FLC, H1-13-318).

2. Letter from Pierre Jeanneret to M. Savoye, 24 August 1929 (FLC, H1-12-66).

Whereas Le Corbusier is taking the lead as public figure, Pierre Jeanneret here takes control of the situation: it is he who clearly follows up the technical process of the construction site, something that is reflected in the numerous letters from his hand to the contractor and the client. Weissmann films Pierre Jeanneret at several moments of discussion with the contractor, on an issue of the hollow floor pots for example, but also with a plan of details of the ledges and beams with the window frames drawn by Albert Frey in May. The captured situations are far removed from the naive optimism of the collaborators from some months before; discussions and creating solutions for the complications are now at the heart of the concerns.

After seven months of structural works, the building entered the year 1930; plasterwork on the façades and tiling were in progress for the Villa as well as for the gardener's house, the works on the surroundings could start but some complications persisted – such as the stability and the mechanics of some window frames and water infiltration. But these difficulties could not stop the enthusiasm of the architects looking forward to the completion of the construction. Weissmann captures two other building-site visits that year in the company of Sigfried Giedion. A fanatical photographer himself, the latter had already visited the construction site of the Villa Savoye in June 1929 – one month after the first reels by Weissmann – accompanied by Christian Zervos, Le Corbusier, and Pierre Jeanneret, during which he took a few photographs. When he returned to Paris during the winter of 1930, Giedion would again visit the now nearly completed building with the aim of publishing an article in *Cahiers d'art*, the art magazine Zervos had founded in 1926 and for which Giedion provided the modern architecture articles. Weissmann accompanies them, and captures on film how Giedion is, with full enthusiasm, approaching the building. The overall chaos and dirtiness of the building site, compounded by the gloomy weather, did not stop Weissmann from taking a panorama of the state of the Villa, although it is hard to see here a convincing building. It is not surprising that Zervos refused to publish almost all the grey photos that Giedion took during that visit, using instead professional photographs that became available for Giedion's article, "Le Corbusier et l'architecture contemporaine".[3] At the very end of construction, in May 1930, Giedion returned to Paris with his wife, Carola Welcker, for another visit to the Villa Savoye, accompanied by Le Corbusier; Pierre Jeanneret; Ernest Weissmann; and Christian Zervos and his future wife, Yvonne Marion. It is a very happy, sunny spring day, and the Villa shines joyfully its victory as a white cube on the grass. The film sequences of Weissmann are this time very close to the photographic viewpoints of Giedion, which suggests that they wandered around the building together. During these two site visits of January and May, the gardener's house also comes to the filmmakers' attention: a small construction close to the Maisons Loucheur typology presenting the architects' statements on social housing, which Weissmann films from the outside, still under construction in January and finished in May. At the same moment, Giedion takes the only photographs of the interiors that today document its original state. Both place particular attention on the wall of rubble stones before the gardener's house, which would introduce new architectural ideas that would be further developed during the 1930s. The enthusiasm for the site reflects the widely

3. Sigfried Giedion, "Le Corbusier et l'architecture contemporaine", *Cahiers d'art*, 1930, 204–215.

The Villa Savoye just completed, arrival at a distance through the trees, photographed by Sigfried Giedion in May 1930 while walking around the site with Ernest Weissmann

shared interest in the project at the time of its realization. It also demonstrates Le Corbusier's constant concern for documenting his works in the various stages of their execution. Weissmann's last filmed footage of the Villa in May 1930 closely corresponds to the commissioning by the Atelier of a series of professional photographs by Marius Gravot in June 1930.

Over the different film footage of the site visits, several methods of filming recur. Besides the importance of the visiting aspect as an event in itself, Weissmann films the progress of the construction with a double gaze: moving panoramic shots, giving a general idea of the progress of the site work, and detailed shots with a focus on specific execution subjects. The early panoramas are difficult to view as film as the movements go from left to right, and sometimes backwards to combine with a movement in height. He is not the only amateur struggling with this; the magazine *Le cinéma chez soi* warns the amateur filmmaker of the panorama as an enemy:

> Disillusionment! The little scene that was perfect in lighting becomes impossible and dizzying on the screen. Looking at it, one is almost dizzy and, besides, the projection is blurred. The horizontal "spinning" is more unpleasant than any error in the diaphragm or the lighting of the subject.[4]

4. Lucien Pierron, "La Prise de Vues Pathé-Baby", *Le cinéma chez soi*, June–July 1929, 2.

Perspective of the first project of the Villa Savoye, 1928, at the crest of its sloping site, which Le Corbusier would use to illustrate various articles on the house

Weissmann was certainly acting as a non-initiated amateur, but he gradually masters the technique of moving the camera slowly so that the complete architectural object can be understood. These panoramic shots recall, of course, the idea of the Villa as already sketched and discussed by Le Corbusier – as an elevated box put on the slope of nature, with equal façades on each side.

> "Site: magnificent property consisting of a large pasture and orchard forming a dome surrounded by a belt of high trees. The house should not have a frontage. Located at the top of the dome, it must open up to the four horizons".[5]

The filmed panoramas reinforce this idea, as it is very difficult with the scaffolding to distinguish the different façades under construction.

Weissmann also focuses on technical details and the execution by the workers. His attention to detail must have given Le Corbusier a valuable record of what he considered to be his major building work of the period. But one could also argue that the complications that occurred during execution were another reason to document as much as possible of the construction. The interest and importance in filming this construction site, as an "internal" document, is also reflected in a series of photographs for use on the construction of the Villa, with some framing and subjects similar to the filmed shots.[6] The importance Le Corbusier attached to photographic records of the construction site seems strange at first glance if one recalls the architect's general reluctance to capture his building sites – not only for the pre-war *œuvre* but even during the construction of his post-war buildings. This aversion is

5. Boesiger, Willy and Oscar Stonorov, eds. *Le Corbusier et Pierre Jeanneret. Œuvre complète 1910-1929*. Third edition, 1943. (Zurich: Girsberger, 1930), 186.

6. Building site photographs, FLC, L2-17-194 to 204, of May 1929 and winter 1930.

Photographs of the Villa Savoye building site published in 1932 in *L'Architecture vivante*, among the image plates of the professional photographs of the finished building

to be understood as a general ban on the circulation of visual documents that could not be controlled by Le Corbusier. The number of construction photographs that were taken is, however, larger than is generally assumed, and publications include construction photographs. These were often realized by Pierre Jeanneret, and so managed by the Atelier itself. Two photographs of the Villa Savoye under construction, probably taken by Jeanneret during a site visit, were published full-page in an edition of the luxury magazine *L'Architecture vivante* edited by Le Corbusier's friend Jean Badovici, among the other professional photographs, drawings, and plans.[7] However, these photographs do not focus on the technical aspects of execution but instead put forward viewpoints that represent the idea of the architecture, as already drawn in perspective sketches by Le Corbusier during the design phase. As such, they are not images of a construction but mentally constructed architecture!

7. Jean Badovici, ed., *L'Architecture vivante. Le Corbusier et P. Jeanneret. Cinquième Série* (Paris: Éditions Albert Morancé, 1932).

Le Corbusier with workers on the building site of the Unité d'Habitation in Marseilles, photographed by Lucien Hervé, 1950

The documenting by Weissmann of the construction of the Villa Savoye over time on film probably ripened in Le Corbusier's mind the idea of commissioning in 1931 not only a series of photographs by Marius Gravot of the building site of the Cité de Refuge[8] but also the planning of a professional film by Pierre Chenal, who was to follow the building site for a period of one year.[9] If the images of the Weissmann reels allowed the unfolding of an unknown story behind the iconic object of the Villa and the discovery of the entire construction process in all its complexity, one of the key projects of Le Corbusier, the Unité d'Habitation in Marseilles, is a completely different story. The images of its construction site between 1948 and 1952 were abundantly published – on the one hand in images controlled by Le Corbusier but, due to the social aspect of the building, also

8. FLC, L2-4-11 to 31.

9. Letter from Pierre Chenal to Le Corbusier, 10 June 1931 (FLC, B3-10-11).

in images that circulated in more regional newspapers. In contrast to a hidden holiday villa in the suburbs of Paris, the project in Marseilles needed this visual propaganda – even more so because of the backlash the construction faced. Le Corbusier appealed again to film, first with the photographer and filmmaker René Zuber to document the evolution on the construction site and later with his advocate, Gabriel Chereau, who realized in 1950-1951 the film *Le Corbusier travaille*,[10] which shows Le Corbusier on the building site of the Marseilles project with his collaborators and the workers. The film emphasizes the humanism behind the big construction, literally giving a face to the architecture – a notion that Lucien Hervé would also highlight in some of his very famous photographs of Le Corbusier on the construction site of the Unité d'Habitation. Le Corbusier's interest in recording in photography and film the construction sites of these three key works moves from amateur recordings for the Villa Savoye to a professionalization through two distinct commissions to a professional photographer and filmmaker for the Cité de Refuge, to a multitude of photographers and filmmakers – both amateur and professional – documenting and communicating the evolution of the Unité d'Habitation. If films on the construction of the key projects in the career of Le Corbusier did indeed become part of his vision of communication strategies for his architecture, this was probably due to the excitement and follow-up on film by Weissmann, which allowed Le Corbusier to realize the potential of communication during construction and how film could pass on a general knowledge of his work.

Le Corbusier and his collaborators filmed by Gabriel Chereau at the building site of the Unité d'Habitation in Marseilles, 1950

10. Gabriel Chereau, dir., *Le Corbusier travaille*, 35 mm, silent documentary, 1951.

On the way to Poissy, a journey of more than one hour's drive from Paris, in the Rolls-Royce of Josep Lluís Sert

Kunio Maekawa, Norman Rice, and Josep Lluís Sert stretching his legs across to Ernest Weissmann, while they are taking photographs of the building site

A filmed panorama of the Villa Savoye under construction in May 1929 shows that building has reached the first floor, with the scaffolding, the temporary ramp, piles of cement, and bricks on site.

Six workmen with their shovels do together the hard work of mixing the concrete from a pile of cement, with water and aggregate.

The frank openness of the workmen on the building site, portrayed by Ernest Weissmann, is striking: he sees them as his equals.

The first floor under construction, with its pots and rebars not yet covered and smoothed with concrete, and a pile of pots in the foreground as “protagonist”

Workman smooth the concrete poured on the pots of the flooring; Ernest Weissmann deliberately chooses a lower viewpoint to focus on the workers rather than the technique.

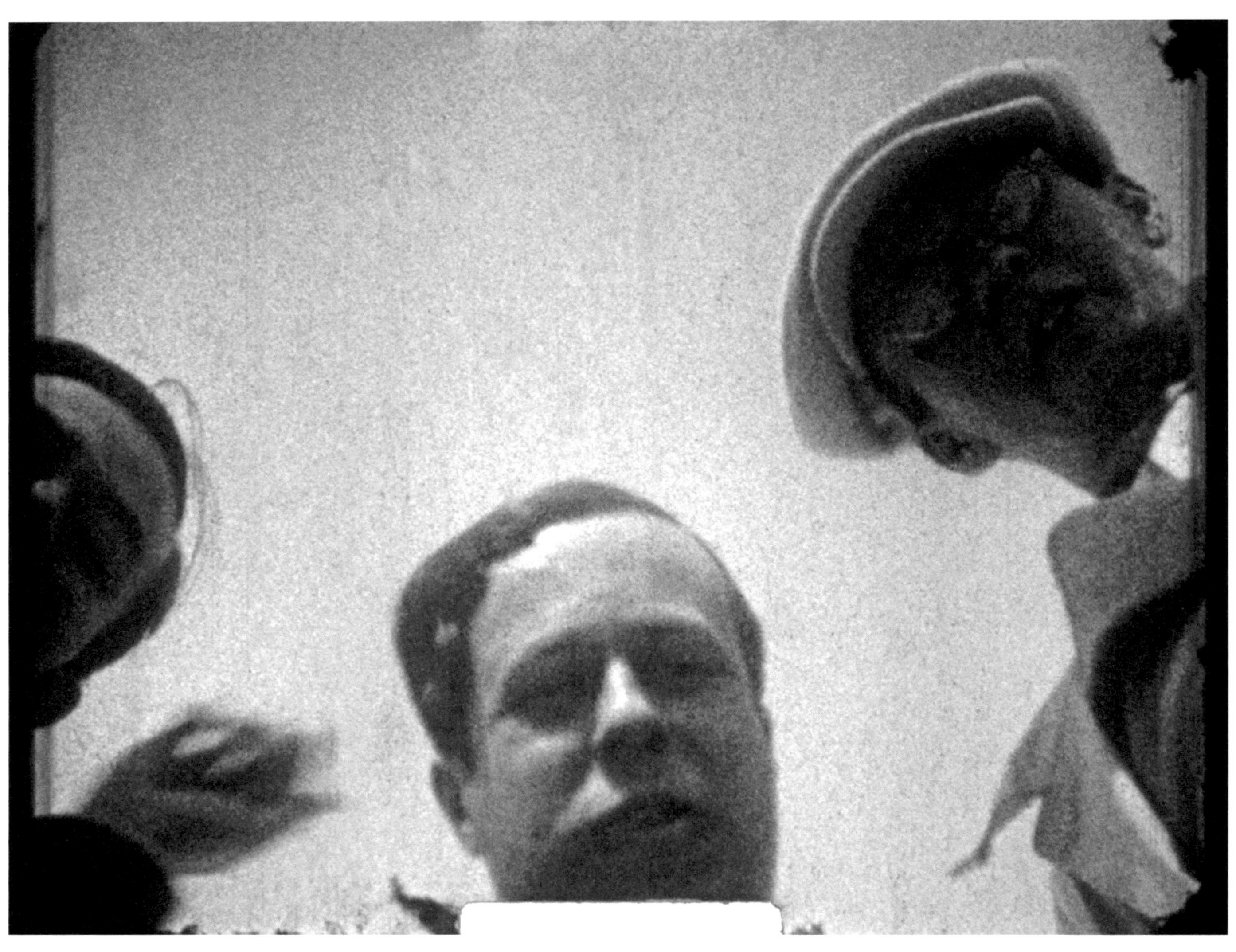

Having fun among friends: Ernest Weissmann films, from ground level, the heads of Kunio Maekawa, Josep Lluís Sert, and Norman Rice.

Josep Lluís Sert, distinguishable by his hat, laughing down the ladder to Ernest Weissmann

Summer 1929: the construction of the villa progresses at great pace;
the floor and the walls of the roof terrace are already constructed.

Workmen bring up the concrete with a pulley to pour it on the pots of the second floor. By getting to a higher level on the construction, the wide view of surrounding nature becomes apparent.

Pierre Jeanneret explains to the contractor and a workman
the details of beams and columns drawn by the Atelier.

Ernest Weissmann films in detail a workman realizing the curved masonry walls of the solarium.

Pierre Jeanneret and Le Corbusier inspecting the works on the first floor, amidst the stanchions for the second floor and the shuttering planks of the columns

This view is from the main terrace to the future living room: masons are working on the curved walls of the solarium, but the walls of the living room are not yet executed. Pierre Jeanneret, at left, is in discussion with a workman; at right, we see Eugene Rosenberg and Le Corbusier.

Ernest Weissmann filmed several times the flowers in the field around the construction site – here, during summer, the poppies.

Sigfried Giedion walking to the almost finished white cube of the Villa Savoye during his visit in winter 1930

May 1930: the Villa Savoye nears completion!
Ernest Weissmann and Sigfried Giedion together cross the site to fully admire the white, elevated “box”.

Sigfried Giedion and his wife, Carola Welcker, caught by Weissmann in a joyful moment, both smiling to each other with the gardener's house in the background

All together! Moments of Mediterranean delight in Athens, 1933

From 29 July until 13 August 1933, the scheduled fourth congress of the CIAM on "The Functional City" takes place as a cruise from Marseilles to Athens, with the official congress being held at the College of Technology in Athens and comprising an exhibition, lectures, touristic excursions, and resolutions formulated during the journey back to Marseilles. Weissmann brings his camera to Athens but does not film the congress itself; instead, he focuses on the joyful reunion with his close friends, wonderment at the constructions on the Acropolis, and the animated farewell of the *Patris II* cruise at the port of Athens where Weissmann boards as a stowaway. Unofficially boarding the cruise becomes almost a metaphor for the non-captured professional importance the congress had for Weissmann and his leftist friends.

Ernest Weissmann had already joined CIAM II at Frankfurt am Main in 1929, and followed from the sidelines the preparations for CIAM III in Brussels the next year, but will only fully engage in CIAM by preparing CIAM IV and attending the congress. The outgoing trip from Marseilles on the *Patris II* cruise was a fruitful prequel, in which the different CIAM members showed and discussed on the boat the panels and reports they had prepared for the exhibition in Athens. However, Weissmann missed this enthusiastic start of the congress on the cruise, where among the hundred participants Le Corbusier and Pierre Jeanneret and his close friends and allies were present, as he arrived in Athens from Croatia by train. For Weissmann – as for his communist friends Josep Lluís Sert, Charlotte Perriand, Pierre Jeanneret, and Wells Coates – the congress had to be the moment of renewal of a political engagement, which had been brought to an end after CIAM III with the departure of several leftist CIAM members to the USSR. Through unofficial conversations and discussions, Weissmann would try to influence the resolutions adopted for the congress in order to shift the focus from the universal model of the functional city, considered by the organizing committee to be the core business, to the broader tasks of architecture and urban design to construct society – including on a political level. But none of these professional activities of the congress was captured by Weissmann on film, in contrast to the enthusiastic sequences of his professional life he had filmed in 1929 and 1930 in Paris. Here, he films the streets around his hotel in Athens and the sights seen on a visit to the Acropolis, the boarding of the *Patris II*, the relaxed atmosphere on the cruise, and the arrival in Marseilles as joyful activities that mask the important professional agenda he had in joining the congress in Athens.

Whereas with the earlier captured moments with Le Corbusier, Pierre Jeanneret, and his friends in 1929 and 1930 in Paris, when his camera was a unique "must-have", in Athens Weissmann is far from being the only person with a camera! The best-known images are shot by László Moholy-Nagy with his Kinamo, on an official mission requested by Sigfried Giedion to document the whole congress trip, which resulted in his film *Architect's Diary*. The accent lays more emphasis on the trip than being a promotional tool for the CIAM itself, as Moholy-Nagy had already announced his approach for making a film as a record of the congress by

Le Corbusier introducing the presentations of the panels of city plans on the *Patris II* by the national delegates

wanting to portray the faces and the expressions of the CIAM members. The Swiss architect Carl Hubacher also came equipped with a camera, a 35mm Leica; Giedion and Jeanneret both brought their photographic cameras; and so did many other architects on the trip – even those of the younger generation: Sert also brought his photographic camera. The event of the congress in Athens (with lectures by Le Corbusier, Cornelius van Eesteren, and others) is almost absent in all the visual mementoes of the members, who prefer to immortalize their gathering together and their exceptional visits to remnants of the ancient culture rather than the professional reasons for their trip. The amateur sequences of Weissmann read as a complement to the better-known images of Moholy-Nagy of how the younger generation perceived the whole gathering, becoming themselves the new active members in record time.

The photographs the different members take during their excursion to the Acropolis – including the footage of Weissmann – show their admiration for the ancient heritage of the Mediterranean. Half of the footage Weissmann films at the congress covers the excursion to the Acropolis. If in the first sequence he films his friends who walked ahead of him in elation, amongst them Sert and Moncha, for all the further sequences Weissmann only has eyes for the beauty of the architecture, the materiality, and the scale of its surroundings. No "family footage" any longer,

The CIAM members during their visit to the Acropolis

but pure excitement for the monuments. Most of the sequences are filmed as panoramas to allow Weissmann to capture the vastness of the site and to combine the different scales of the Acropolis, taking in the details of the columns, their materiality, their form, the shadows on their arrises and on the foreground – all of that with the other temples and the city of Athens in the background of this visual feast. Through the filmed sequences, one can perceive the trajectory of their walk through the site. Weissmann first films upwards a panorama while entering the Propylaea, then turns his view to film, through its columns, the temple of Athena Nikè, a panorama of the Erechtheion with the Propylaea in the background, a close-up of the caryatids, and finally ends at the Parthenon. The Parthenon sequence is very short, as Weissmann probably ran out of film. The sequences read like a visual translation of what Giedion wrote in *Cahiers d'art* in 1934, in which he describes the feeling of the columns as "something alive",[1] but Weissmann's filming approach also evokes Giedion's vision of some years earlier on the necessity of filming modern architecture instead of photographing it – according to him, the only possibility to reveal the essence of the architecture.[2] Weissmann's astonishment at seeing the ancient Greek constructions recalls the experience of Le Corbusier more than 20 years earlier during his journey "in the East", when, in September 1911, he spent three weeks with his friend August Klipstein on the Acropolis immersing himself in the overwhelming truth and

1. Sigfried Giedion, "Pallas Athéné ou le visage de la Grèce", *Cahiers d'art*, 1934, 77–80.

2. Sigfried Giedion, *Bauen in Frankreich - Bauen in Eisen - Bauen in Eisenbeton* (Leipzig/Berlin: Klinkhardt & Biermann, 1928), 176.

harmony of the architecture on site. Le Corbusier later refers to a "pure creation of the mind" in 1922 and in 1923 in his article in *L'Esprit nouveau* and in *Vers une architecture*, where he covers in more than 20 pages his ideas on the temples at the Acropolis, illustrated with photographs that he took from the collection *L'Image de la Grèce* of the famous photographer Fred Boissonnas.[3] About the Propylaea, he recalls the complete harmony of the elements:

> What does emotion arise from? From a certain relationship between categorical elements: cylinders, polished floor, polished walls. From a concordance with the things of the site. From a plastic system that extends its effects to every part of the composition. A unity of ideas from the unity of the material to the unity of the moderation[4]

Sketch by Le Corbusier of the view of the Parthenon through the columns of the Propylaea, 1911

Almost a week after the Acropolis visit, Weissmann films the departure of the *Patris II* back to Marseilles. First, sequences are shot at the quay at Piraeus port, showing the arrival of all CIAM members – and one can again distinguish amongst others Le Corbusier, who is followed as a star, but also Jeanneret, Sert, and Moncha. These sequences are an introduction for the little *mise en scène* that will follow. While someone is filming, Weissmann and his friends embark on the *Patris II* cruise. They all wave to the camera, standing at the railing of the boat, suggesting their departure. One could suppose at first sight that it is Weissmann waving goodbye from the harbour quay, leaving his friends returning by boat and himself returning as he arrived by train from Croatia, but he is joining his friends on the trip back to Marseilles as a stowaway – not for pleasure but because of wanting to intervene in the final writing of the resolutions of the congress. This act is taken as the occasion to testify on film how he gets on board, and the sequence is almost an allegory for his active involvement in CIAM, in reply to Giedion's remark from late

3. Fred Boissonnas, *L'Image de la Grèce. Athènes ancienne* (Geneva: Éditions d'Art Boissonnas, 1921).

4. Le Corbusier, *Vers une architecture*, Collection de "L'Esprit Nouveau" (Paris: Les Éditions G. Crès & Cie, 1923), 117.

172 VERS UNE ARCHITECTURE

PARTHÉNON. — Système plastique.

ARCHITECTURE, PURE CRÉATION DE L'ESPRIT 173

PARTHÉNON. — Voici la machine à émouvoir. Nous entrons dans l'implacable de la mécanique. Il n'est pas de symboles attachés à ces formes ; ces formes provoquent des sensations catégoriques ; plus besoin d'une clé pour comprendre. Du brutal, de l'intense, du plus doux, du très fin, du très fort. Et qui a trouvé la composition de ces éléments ? Un inventeur génial. Ces cailloux étaient inertes dans les carrières du Pentélique, informes. Pour les grouper ainsi, il ne fallait pas être ingénieur ; il fallait être un grand sculpteur.

Double page of *Vers une architecture*, from the chapter "Pure Creation of the Mind", 172–173

1930, "we do not just need your appearance, but also active collaboration. What do you think about this?"[5] The fatigue and relaxed atmosphere on the trip back filmed by Moholy-Nagy, and also by Weissmann, is hence only for appearance's sake – and masks the differences between the members in the writing of the resolutions of the congress. In fact, Weissmann submitted an alternative proposal that was supported by the leftist young architects – among them Sert, Perriand, Coates, and others – to the one that was drafted by the resolution committee, which included in the first place Le Corbusier and Van Eesteren. Weissmann, Sert, and Coates also worked on this official proposal, trying to influence the resolutions as much as possible with their communist political convictions regarding the necessity of the reorganization of land and property. This was in complete opposition to the convictions of Le Corbusier and others, for whom their actions should be limited to their areas of expertise – architecture and urban design – remaining apolitical.

Arriving in Marseilles by sea is again for Weissmann the opportunity to take up the camera and to film large panoramas of the sea and the port, before getting

5. Letter from Sigfried Giedion to Ernest Weissmann, 5 November 1930, in: Tamara Bjažić Klarin, *Ernest Weissmann: Društveno Angažirana Arhitektura, 1926.- 1939/ Socially Engaged Architecture, 1926-1939* (Zagreb: Hrvatska akademija znanosti i umjetnosti, 2015), 180.

back to work to finalize the resolutions after Le Corbusier's departure. When Le Corbusier received the latest versions of the resolutions written in Marseilles, he was furious and accused Weissmann and his friends of being cowards, cheating and dealing behind his back:

> The congress was "delightful", youthful, active. It seemed to end on a winning note. It was me who gave it [the resolutions]. Alas, today I receive the last draft which was made on arrival in Marseille by the young people. I had insisted on slipping away to give [a] free hand [to them]. It is a complete deflation! The young people! The young people? What a beautiful word. In fact – I always say it – everyone is young once in his life, and that means nothing in the field of action and thought. You become young later, or you grow old. Young people are shy when they are not cowards. I will react harshly and strongly[6]

Le Corbusier's reaction clearly shows how he still had in mind his young collaborators of four years ago. When Weissmann acquired his camera at that time, he and his close friends were young, enthusiastic to absorb from the masters, and he filmed that professional environment. In Athens, by contrast, the professional intentions and work are separated from the leisure, and no longer immortalized on film. But at the same time, these events affirm the professionalization of this new generation, becoming fully part of the architectural scene and wanting to take the lead as equals of their masters.

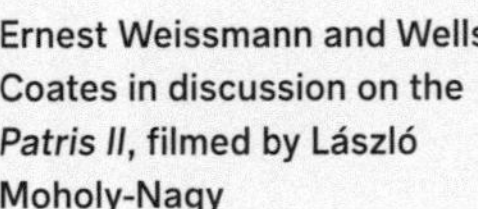

Ernest Weissmann and Wells Coates in discussion on the *Patris II*, filmed by László Moholy-Nagy

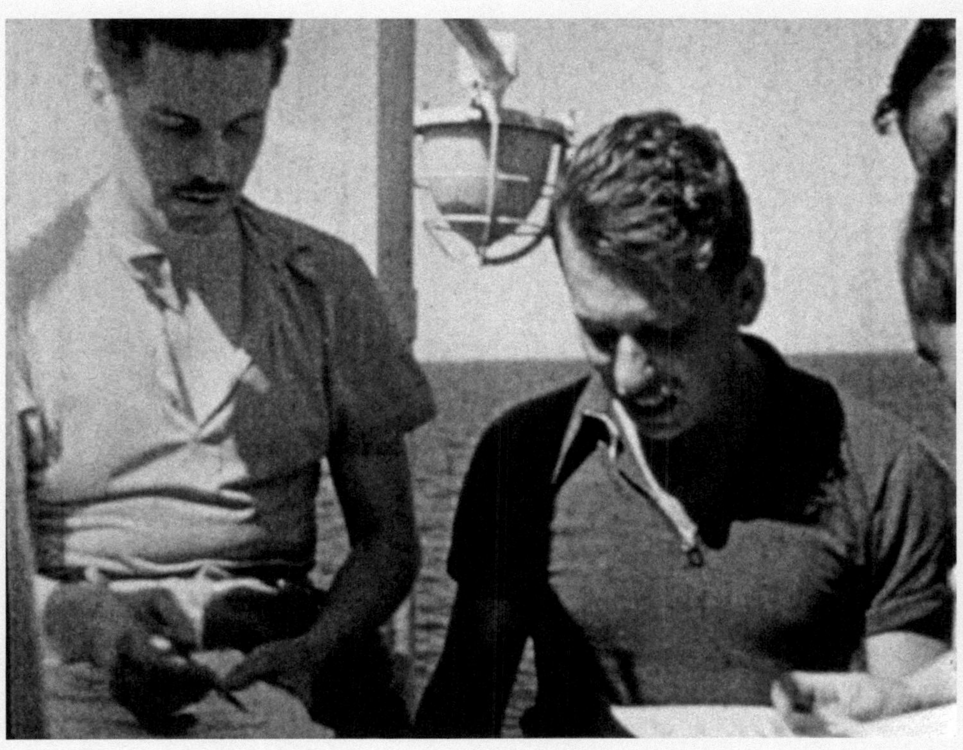

6. Letter from Le Corbusier to his mother, 28 August 1933, in: Le Corbusier, Rémi Baudouï, and Arnaud Dercelles, *Correspondance. Lettres à la famille. Tome II: 1926-1946* (Gollion: Infolio, 2013), 446.

Josep Lluís Sert and Moncha in the middle, with
two other friends, walking to the Acropolis

The Propylaea – starting point of the visit to the
Acropolis and start of a panoramic sequence

Different scales and depths at the Propylaea, with, in the foreground, blocks of the columns of the Parthenon

A view through from the Erechtheion, with some of
the other CIAM members in the portal opening

A close-up of the caryatids (then still original, today replaced by copies), filmed from below

Start of a panoramic view of the Erechtheion,
showing the caryatid porch

The *Patris II* cruise at the port of Piraeus, just before boarding

A sailor in full costume at the port of Piraeus

All CIAM members arrive at the port of Piraeus for the departure to Marseilles. Ernest Weissmann follows with his camera the arrival of Le Corbusier (with hat and cigarette) as a star surrounded by architects.

Le Corbusier in the middle of the attention, between
two women with hats admiring the architect

Boarding the *Patris II*: the blackboard indicates time of departure, just above Charlotte Perriand at the rail smiling to the camera.

Ernest Weissmann, Alfred Roth, Moncha, and another friend boarded on the *Patris II* and leaning on the ship's rail.

About the main actors

Le Corbusier (1887–1965) is considered one of the most famous visionary architects and urban designers of the 20th century. With his cousin, he ran the Atelier Le Corbusier and Pierre Jeanneret from 1922 until 1940. During this period, most of the practice's modernist villas were built, and bigger works such as the Centrosoyus in Moscow, and the Cité de Refuge and the Pavillon Suisse in Paris, realized. In parallel, Le Corbusier developed urban-design projects for such cities as Paris, Antwerp, Algiers, and Buenos Aires, and wrote extensively on his architectural and urbanistic ideas. He continued the Atelier Le Corbusier on an individual base from 1940 on, with projects such as the Unités d'Habitation in Marseilles and in Nantes-Rezé, Briey, Firminy, and Berlin; the Monastery of Sainte-Marie de La Tourette; and the church of Notre-Dame du Haut Ronchamp. He designed the new state capital of the north Indian states of Punjab and Haryana, Chandigarh, with its representative buildings, from 1951 on.

Pierre Jeanneret (1896–1967) was a Swiss architect who, together with Le Corbusier, led the Atelier Le Corbusier and Pierre Jeanneret from 1922 until 1940. He collaborated with Jean Prouvé, Charlotte Perriand, and Georges Blanchon on industrialized processes for houses in series, and had his own independent architecture practice with projects such as the Centre d'apprentissage at Béziers. From 1951 until 1966, he was the on-site architect in Chandigarh for Le Corbusier, and realized numerous houses and other buildings for the new city.

Ernest Weissmann (1903–1985) was a Croatian (then-Yugoslav) architect and developer/planner. He graduated in architecture in Zagreb, and worked for Adolf Loos and Le Corbusier and Pierre Jeanneret in Paris. He dedicated his work to the development of the prefabricated hospital-building type and city planning viewed from social and economic points of view. He was an active member of the Congrès Internationaux d'Architecture Moderne (CIAM) from 1929 until 1947. From 1942 until 1966, he worked for the United States Board of Economic Warfare and United Nations Relief and Rehabilitation Administration, Economic Commission, and Department of Economic and Social Affairs. At the UN, Weissmann was in charge of housing, building, and planning at a global scale.

Index of names

Bibliography

Contemporary literature

Alonso Pereira, José Ramon. "Le Corbusier's dioramas". *Cuadernos de Proyectos Arquitectonicos*, no. 4 (2013): 133–135.

Amirante, Roberta, Burcu Kütükçüoglu, Panayotis Tournikiotis, and Yannis Tsiomis, eds. *L'invention d'un architecte: le voyage en Orient de Le Corbusier*. Paris: Éditions de la Villette, 2013.

Arzoumanian, Varoujan and Patrick Bardou, eds. *Le Corbusier et la Méditerranée*. Marseilles: Editions Parenthèses : Musées de Marseilles, 1987.

Bacon, Mardges. *Le Corbusier in America*. Cambridge, Massachusetts: MIT Press, 2001.

Bedarida, Marc. "Une journée au 35 S". In *Le Corbusier, moments biographiques: XIVe rencontres*, edited by Fondation Le Corbusier and Roger Aujame, 26–51. Paris: La Villette, 2008.

Benton, Tim. *Les villas parisiennes de Le Corbusier et Pierre Jeanneret, 1920-1930: L'invention de la maison moderne*. Philippe Sers, 1984. Paris: Éditions de La Villette 2007.

Benton, Tim. *LC Foto: Le Corbusier: Secret Photographer*. Zurich: Lars Müller, 2013.

Bjažić Klarin, Tamara. *Ernest Weissmann: društveno angažirana arhitektura, 1926-1939/Socially Engaged Architecture, 1926-1939*. Zagreb: Hrvatska akademija znanosti i umjetnosti, 2015.

Bjažić Klarin, Tamara. "Ernest Weissmann's Architectural and Planning Practices. Continuity of Original Concerns of 'New Architecture' and Post-car Reconstruction". *Prostor*, 63 (2022): 2–13.

Blencowe, Chris and Judith Levine. *Moholy's Edit: The Avant-Garde at Sea, August 1933*. Zurich: Lars Müller, 2019.

Boone, Veronique and Bénédicte Gandini. "Exploring the Visual Material within the Building Process of the Villa Savoye". In *Building Knowledge, Constructing Histories. Proceedings of the 6th International Congress on Construction History*, edited by Ine Wouters, Stéphanie Van de Voorde, Ine Bertels, Bernard Espion, and Krista de Jonge, 373–382. Leiden: CRC Press/Balkema, 2018.

Burri, René and Arthur Rüegg. *Le Corbusier: Photographs by René Burri/Magnum: Moments in the Life of a Great Architect*. Basel: Birkhäuser Verlag, 1999.

Caroux, Hélène, Benoît Pouvreau, and Antoine Furio. *L'aéroport du Bourget entre les lignes: histoire d'un territoire en Seine-Saint-Denis*. Bobigny: Conseil départemental de la Seine-Saint-Denis, 2015.

Cauquil, Hélène and Marc Bedarida. "Le Corbusier. L'Atelier 35 Rue de Sèvres". *Bulletin d'information architecturale de l'Institut Français d'Architecture*, supplement to no. 114, Summer 1987.

Charollais, Isabelle and André Ducret, eds. *Le Corbusier à Genève, 1922-1932: projets et réalisations*. Lausanne: Payot, 1987.

Cohen, Jean-Louis. *Le Corbusier et la mystique de l'U.R.S.S.* Brussels: Mardaga, 1987.

Cohen, Jean-Louis. "Moment suspendus: le voyage aérien et les métaphores volantes". In *Le Corbusier, moments biographiques: XIVe rencontres*, edited by Fondation Le Corbusier, 144–157. Paris: La Villette, 2008.

Delhomme, Jean-Philippe and Jean-Marc Savoye. *The Sunny Days of Villa Savoye*. Basel: Birkhäuser, 2020.

Difford, Richard. "Infinite Horizons: Le Corbusier, the Pavilion de l'Esprit Nouveau Dioramas and the Science of Visual Distance". *The Journal of Architecture*, Vol. 14, no. 3 (2009): 295–323.

Folino, Antonietta. *Otlet-Le Corbusier: lettere sulla costruzione della Cité mondiale (1927-1934). enumera 6.* Ariccia: Aracne, 2016.

Galić, Drago, ed. "Ernest Weissmann". *Rad HAZU*, 437 (1991): 92–97.

Gillen, Jacques, Stéphanie Manfroid, and Raphaèle Cornille, eds. *Paul Otlet: fondateur du Mundaneum (1868-1944): architecte du savoir, artisan de paix*. Hors collection. Brussels: Impressions nouvelles, 2010.

Gourdet-Mares, Anne. "La Caméra Pathé-Baby: le cinéma amateur à l'âge de l'expérimentation". In *L'amateur de cinéma: un autre paradigme: histoire, esthétique, marges et institutions*, edited by Valérie Vignaux and Benoît Turquety, Histoire culturelle. Paris: Afrhc, 2017.

Gourdet-Mares, Anne and Elvira Shahmiri. *Pathé-Baby. Le cinéma chez soi*. Paris: Édition Fondation Jérôme Seydoux-Pathé, 2022.

Gresleri, Giuliano. *Le Corbusier, Voyage d'Orient. Charles-Edouard Jeanneret, photographe et écrivain*. Paris: Fondation Le Corbusier, 1984.

Gresleri, Giuliano and Dario Matteoni. *La Citta' Mondiale*. Quaderni di Architettura e Urbanistica, 28. Venezia: Polis/Marsilio Editori, 1982.

Grunewald, Almut, Bronwen Saunders, Sigfried Giedion, and Carola Giedion-Welcker, eds. *The Giedion World: Sigfried Giedion and Carola Giedion-Welcker in Dialogue*. Zurich: Scheidegger & Spiess, 2019.

Huhtamo, Erkki. *Illusions in motion: media archaeology of the moving panorama and related spectacles*. Leonardo book series. Cambridge, Massachusetts: MIT Press, 2013.

Le Corbusier. *Carnets 1, 1914-1948*. Edited by Maurice Besset, Françoise de Franclieu, and Fondation Le Corbusier. Paris: Herscher/Dessain et Tolra, 1981.

Le Corbusier, Rémi Baudouï, and Arnaud Dercelles. *Correspondance. Lettres à la famille. Tome II: 1926-1946*. Gollion: Infolio, 2013.

Levie, Françoise and Benoît Peeters. *L'homme qui voulait classer le monde: Paul Otlet et le Mundaneum*. Réflexions faites. Brussels: Impressions nouvelles, 2006.

Mazza, Barbara. *Le Corbusier e la fotografia. La vérité blanche*. Florence: Firenze University Press, 2002.

Mellegers, Ernie J. *9079 U 2. Le Corbusier en de auto*. Rotterdam: Mellegers, 1992.

Mumford, Eric. *The CIAM discourse on urbanism, 1928-1960*. Cambridge, Massachusetts: MIT Press, 2000.

Odin, Roger. "La question de l'amateur dans trois espaces de réalisation et de diffusion". *Communications*, 68, 'Le cinéma en amateur' (1999): 47–89.

Oechslin, Werner and Gregor Harbusch, eds. *Sigfried Giedion und die Fotografie. Bildinszenierungen der Moderne*. Zurich: gta Verlag, 2010.

Olmo, Carlo and Susanna Caccia. *La villa Savoye. Icona, rovina, restauro (1948-1968)*. Rome: Donzelli editore, 2017.

Ortiz Dos Santos, Daniela. "Routes of Modernity or the Americas of Le Corbusier. Voyages, Affinities and Anthropophagy". Doctoral dissertation in Sciences, ETH Zurich, 2017.

Perriand, Charlotte. *Une vie de création*. Paris: Odile Jacob, 1998.

Quetglas, Josep. *Les Heures Claires. Proyecto y arquitectura en la villa Savoye de Le Corbusier y Pierre Jeanneret*. Sant Cugat del Vallès: Associació d'Idees, Centre d'Investigacions Estètiques, 2009.

Rascaroli, Laura, Barry Monahan, and Gwenda Young, eds. *Amateur filmmaking: the home movie, the archive, the Web*. New York: Bloomsbury Academic, 2014.

Rosa, Joseph. *Albert Frey, architect*. New York: Rizzoli International, 1990.

Rosellini, Anna. "La surface puriste, de 'L'Esprit Nouveau' à la villa Savoye". In *Le Corbusier: l'œuvre à l'épreuve de sa restauration*, 90–101. Collection "Rencontres de la Fondation Le Cobusier". Paris: Éditions de la Villette : Fondation Le Corbusier, 2017.

Rovira i Gimeno, Josep M. *José Luis Sert, 1901-1983*. Milan: Electa Architecture, 2003.

Sbriglio, Jacques. *Le Corbusier: La Villa Savoye. The Villa Savoye*. Basel: Birkhäuser, 1999.

Schildt, Göran. *Alvar Aalto. The Decisive Years*. New York: Rizzoli, 1986.

Somer, Kees and Ed Taverne. *The Functional City: The CIAM and Cornelis van Eesteren, 1928-1960*. Rotterdam: nai010 Publishers, 2007.

Tolić, Ines, "Ernest Weissmann's 'World City'. The Reconstruction of Skopje within the Cold War Context". *Southeastern Europe*, 2 (2017): 171–199.

Van Es, Evelien, Gregor Harbusch, and Muriel Perez. *Atlas of the Functional City: CIAM 4 and Comparative Urban Analysis*. Bussum: Thoth publishers, 2014.

Van Sande, Hera. "Kunio Maekawa. A Japanese Modernist in Search for Architectural Identity". Doctoral thesis in Architectural Engineering, Vrije Universiteit Brussel, 2008.

Vignaux, Valérie and Benoît Turquety, eds. *L'amateur de cinéma: un autre paradigme: histoire, esthétique, marges et institutions*. Histoire culturelle. Paris: Afrhc, 2017.

Historical literature

Badovici, Jean, ed. *L'Architecture vivante. Le Corbusier et P. Jeanneret. Cinquième série*. Paris: Éditions Albert Morancé, 1932.

Boesiger, Willy and Oscar Stonorov, eds. *Le Corbusier et Pierre Jeanneret. Œuvre complète 1910-1929*. Third edition, 1943. Zurich: Girsberger, 1930.

Boesiger, Willy and Oscar Stonorov, eds. *Le Corbusier et Pierre Jeanneret. Œuvre complète 1929-1934*. Zurich: Girsberger, 1935.

de Fayet. "Toepffer, précurseur du cinema". Collection de "L'Esprit Nouveau", no. 11-12. Paris: Les Editions G. Cres & Cie, 1921.

Gardner-Medwin, Robert. "United Nations and Resettlement in the Far East". *The Town Planning Review*, no. 4 (1952): 283–298.

Giedion, Sigfried. *Bauen in Frankreich - Bauen in Eisen - Bauen in Eisenbeton*. Leipzig/Berlin: Klinkhardt & Biermann, 1928.

Giedion, Sigfried. "Le Corbusier et l'architecture contemporaine". *Cahiers d'art* (1930): 204–215.

Giedion, Sigfried. "Pallas Athéné ou le visage de la Grèce". *Cahiers d'art* (1934): 77–80.

Giedion, Sigfried. "CIAM at sea". *Architect's year book* (1949): 36–38.

Goissaud, Anthony. "Le port aérien du Bourget". *La construction moderne* (18 December 1927): 133–144.

L'Architecture d'aujourd'hui, Le Corbusier. *2ème numéro spécial* (2nd special edition), 1948.

Le Corbusier. *Vers une architecture*. Collection de "L'Esprit Nouveau". Paris: Les Éditions G. Crès & Cie, 1923.

Le Corbusier. *Urbanisme*. Collection de "L'Esprit Nouveau". Paris: Les Éditions G. Crès & Cie, 1925.

Le Corbusier. *Almanach d'architecture moderne*. Collection de "L'Esprit Nouveau". Paris: Les Éditions G. Crès & Cie, 1926.

Le Corbusier. *Une maison - un palais. À la recherche d'une unité architecturale*. Collection de "L'Esprit Nouveau". Paris: Les Éditions G. Crès & Cie, 1928.

Le Corbusier. *Précisions sur un état présent de l'architecture et de l'urbanisme*. Paris: Les Éditions G. Crès & Cie, 1930.

Le Corbusier. *Aircraft*. "The New Vision" series. London–New York: The Studio, 1935.

Le Corbusier. *La Ville Radieuse*. Collection de l'équipement de la civilisation machiniste. Boulogne-sur-Seine: Éditions de l'Architecture d'Aujourd'hui, 1935.

Le Corbusier. "The vertical garden city". *Architectural Review*, Vol. 79, no. 475 (January 1936).

Le Corbusier. *Sur les 4 routes*. Paris: Gallimard, 1941.

Le Corbusier. *Manière de penser l'urbanisme*. Urbanisme des CIAM. ASCORAL, first volume. Paris: Éditions de l'Architecture d'Aujourd'hui, 1943.

Le Corbusier and Philippe Duboÿ. *Aircraft*. (London–New York: The Studio, 1935) Marseilles: Parenthèses, facsimile of 2017.

Le Corbusier et le groupe CIAM - France. *La Charte d'Athènes*. Collection de l'équipement de la civilisation machiniste. Boulogne-sur-Seine: Éditions de l'Architecture d'Aujourd'hui, 1943.

"Les lignes Farman". *Les Ailes* (20 June 1929): 9.

Otlet, Paul. *Cité mondiale. Geneva: World Civic Center: Mundaneum*. Vol. 133. Brussels: Union des Associations Internationales, 1929.

Petit, Jean, ed. *Le Corbusier parle*. Micro-Carnets Forces Vives. Paris: Les Éditions Forces Vives, 1967

Pierron, Lucien. "La prise de vues Pathé-Baby". *Le cinéma chez soi* (June–July 1929): 2–3.

Planić, Stjepan. *Problemi savremene arhitekture*. Zagreb: Jugoslovenska štampa, 1932.

Rice, Norman. "I remember 35, rue de Sèvres". *PSA News*, May 1981.

Roth, Alfred. *Begegnung mit Pionieren. Le Corbusier, Piet Mondrian, Adolf Loos, Josef Hoffmann, Auguste Perret, Henry van de Velde*. Basel: Birkhäuser, 1973.

Roth, Alfred. *Amüsante Erlebnisse eines Architekten*. Zurich: gta/Ammann, 1988.

Weissmann, Ernest. "Grave Deficit of Dwellings in Postwar Europe". *Housing and Town and Country Planning. United Nations Bulletin*, 1 (1948): 15–22.

Weissmann, Ernest. "The Role of the UN in Urban Research and Planning". In *Urban Research and Policy Planning*, edited by Leo F. Schnore and Henry Fagin. Vol. I, 553–581. Beverly Hills, California: Sage Publications, 1967.

Weissmann, Ernest (et al.). "Solutions de principe. Rapporteur: Le Corbusier. Conclusion de la commission", 112–115. In *5e Congrès CIAM. Paris 1937. Logis et loisirs*. Boulogne-sur-Seine: L'Architecture d'Aujourd'hui, 1937.

Film and television

Alexander, Alexandre, dir. *Les mains de Paris*. 35 mm, sound documentary. NERO-Films, 1934.

Chenal, Pierre, *Architectures d'aujourd'hui*. 32mm, silent documentary, 1931.

Fouchet, Max-Pol, dir. *Paris à sauver, Paris à reconstruire. Terre des arts*. Sound documentary. ORTF, 7 August 1960.

Gabriel Chereau, dir., *Le Corbusier Travaille*. 35 mm, silent documentary, 1951.

Gertrude Stein home movie. 16mm, amateur film, 1928.

Le Corbusier, *amateur films*. 16mm, amateur film, 1936.

Moholy-Nagy, László, dir. Film diary: *Architects' Congress*, 16mm, silent documentary, 1933.

Prouteau, Gilbert, dir. *Le Corbusier*. 35 mm/16 mm, silent and sound documentary rushes. Tadié Cinéma, 1964.

About the authors

Veronique Boone is an architect from the University of Ghent, Belgium and doctor from the École Nationale Supérieure d'Architecture et de Paysage de Lille (ENSAPL), France and the Université Libre de Bruxelles (ULB), Belgium. She is an associate professor at the Faculty of Architecture La Cambre Horta at the ULB. She lectures on architectural history and theory as well as on the conservation of 20th-century architecture. Her research focuses on the history and theory, as well as alternative narratives of modern architecture. She has published extensively in academic publications on Le Corbusier and the mediation of architecture by film and television, and is a correspondent for Belgian and international architectural magazines on contemporary architecture. She has worked on several exhibitions as curator and/or contributor to catalogues – among them, *Lucien Hervé, l'oeil de l'architecte*, CIVA, 2005; *Le Corbusier and the Power of Photography*, Musée des beaux-arts La Chaux-de-Fonds, 2012; *L'Architecture modern à l'écran*, Cinematek, 2014; *In the Studio at 35, rue de Sèvres: an Amateur cameraman's Informal View*, Fondation Le Corbusier, 2017 and Atelier Jespers, 2018. She is also Vice-President of DOCOMOMO Belgium.

Tim Benton was trained at Cambridge University and the Courtauld Institute of Art. He has taught at the Open University in Milton Keynes since 1970. He has published widely on the history of architecture and design, notably on the interwar period, specializing in the work of Le Corbusier. He currently teaches a doctoral class at the École Polytechnique Fédérale de Lausanne (EPFL), Switzerland. His books include *The Villas of Le Corbusier 1920-1930* (1984, 1987, 2007) and *The Rhetoric of Modernism: Le Corbusier as a Lecturer* (2007, 2008). He has worked on a large number of exhibitions as curator and contributor to catalogues – notably, *Thirties: British Art and Design Before the War*, Hayward Gallery, 1980; *Art and Power: Europe under the Dictators 1930-1945*, South Bank Centre, 1995; *Art Deco 1910-1939*, V&A, 2003; *Modernism: designing a new world 1914-1939*, V&A, 2003; and *Le Corbusier and the Power of Photography*, Musée des beaux-arts La Chaux-de-Fonds, 2012.

Tamara Bjažić Klarin is Senior Research Advisor at the Institute of Art History in Zagreb. She graduated in architecture and received a PhD in History of Art at Zagreb. Her field of expertise is 20th-century urban planning and architectural history, with a focus on knowledge exchange and public engagement by architects. She authored the books *Ernest Weissmann. Socially Engaged Architecture, 1926-39* and *"Za bolji, ljepši Zagreb!" – arhitektonski i urbanistički natječaji međuratnog Zagreba, 1918-1941*. She was an expert advisor for the exhibition *Toward a Concrete Utopia: Architecture in Yugoslavia, 1948–1980*, MoMA, 2018–2019. She has co-authored several TV broadcasts and documentaries on architecture produced by Croatian National Television (with Ana Marija Habjan). In 2014, she was an academic guest at the Institute for the History and Theory of Architecture (gta) at the ETH (Swiss Federal Institute of Technology) in Zurich.

Acknowledgements

My first dept is to Michel Richard, at the time Director of the Fondation Le Corbusier, who offered me the freedom to digitalize the Weissmann films and present an exhibition with enlargements of stills at the Villa La Roche-Jeanneret in Paris in 2017. Merits also go to Jean-François Declercq for his enthusiastic and generous support to repeat and extend the exhibition in Brussels at the Atelier Jespers.

It was thanks to Mary McLeod – who reminded me about the existence of these films that she saw many years earlier, projected at Marc Dessauce's – that my interest was awakened to search for this exceptional material. It was then a small but intriguing side project in the rush of the end of my PhD; I am grateful to Richard Klein for not having lost confidence about my landing on time at the academic level. My full recognition goes to Gordon Weissmann, and the Fondation Le Corbusier and its director Brigitte Bouvier for access to the archives and the reproduction of the images and film stills. I especially thank the archivist Isabelle Godineau and librarian Arnaud Dercelles for always being at my disposal with answers to my questions about archival material. I am highly indebted to Anne Gourdet-Marès of the Fondation Seydoux-Pathé Baby for her endless knowledge on the history of the Pathé Baby.

Numerous experts, colleagues, and friends supported me with discussions and answering my never-ending questioning on details: Hera Van de Sande on Kunio Maekawa, Andreas Kalpakci and Almut Grunewald on Sigfried Giedion, Josep Rovira on Josep Lluís Sert, Martina Hrabová on the Czech and Slovakian collaborators, Kees Somer on CIAM IV, Didier Teissonnier on the workplace of the Atelier, Antoine Furio and Jean-Emmanuel Terrier on Le Bourget, Timo Riekko on Alvar Aalto. With Bénédicte Gandini, I analysed the construction plans of the Villa Savoye; with Raymond Balau, I investigated the intriguing history of the pavilion and the diorama for the Cité Mondiale – and, of course, with Tamara Bjažić Klarin, I held enthusiastic discussions on the life and career of Ernest Weissmann. Michel Barrière and many other amateur collectors on car and plane topics were generous in sharing their knowledge with me; I think in a book that deals with the interest of amateur material, it is appropriate to recognize their lifelong investigation on the most diverse topics. I am grateful to Tim Benton, with whom I share a long interest in Le Corbusier and the visual material, for writing the foreword, and to Tamara Bjažić Klarin, for writing the introduction to Ernest Weissmann. The book wouldn't have been so beautiful without the energy Gunther Fobe put into it. Thomas, Johan, and Hilde gave me endless support while researching and writing the text; this book is dedicated to them.

Illustration credits

© F.L.C. / 2023, ProLitteris, Zurich
all illustrations except the following:

© 1928 – Collection Fondation Jérôme Seydoux-Pathé – Fonds Robert Guenet
p. 12

© 1928 – Collection Fondation Jérôme Seydoux-Pathé
p. 15

© Private Collections
p. 13, p. 51 (below), p. 55 (above), p. 101

© The Ernest Weissmann Archive, Marc Dessauce Collection, Ubu Gallery, New York
p. 14, p. 19, p. 20, p. 21, p. 25, p. 26

© gta Archives, ETH Zurich, CIAM
p. 23

© National and University Library, Zagreb
p. 27

© United Nations, New York (from *Skopje Resurgent*, 1970)
p. 28

© Norman N. Rice Collection, The Architectural Archives, University of Pennsylvania
p. 33

© Succession Alexander Alexander – Collection et restauration du film par le CNC
p. 36 (above)

© GP Archives, Collection Tadié
p. 36 (below)

© Lucien Hervé Photographs Collection, Accession no. 2002.R.14, The Getty Research Institute, Los Angeles, Copyright J. Paul Getty Trust
p. 37, p. 126

© L'Illustré
p. 75

© AACA Library & Research Center, Hershey, Pennsylvania
p. 100

© Archives et Bibliothèque d'Architecture, Université Libre de Bruxelles, Brussels
p. 125

© Gabriel Chereau Collection
p. 127

© gta Archives / ETH Zurich, Karl Hubacher
p. 151

© Collection Van Eesteren, Het Nieuwe Instituut, Rotterdam
p. 152

© Moholy-Nagy Estate
p. 155